THE
TIPPING POINT
How Little Things Can Make a Big Difference

MALCOLM GLADWELL

BACK BAY BOOKS
Little, Brown and Company
NEW YORK   BOSTON

The author is grateful for permission to include the following previously copyrighted material. Excerpts from interviews on Market Mavens videotape by Linda Price, Lawrence F. Feick, and Audrey Guskey. Reprinted by permission of the authors. Excerpts from Daniel Wegner, "Transactive Memory: A Contemporary Analysis of the Group Mind," *Journal of Personality and Social Psychology* (1991), vol. 61, no. 6. Reprinted by permission of the author. Excerpts from Donald H. Rubinstein, "Love and Suffering: Adolescent Socialization and Suicide in Micronesia," *Contemporary Pacific* (Spring 1995), vol. 7, no. 1, and "Epidemic Suicide Among Micronesian Adolescents," *Social Science and Medicine* (1983), vol. 17. Reprinted by permission of the author. Excerpts from *Paul Revere's Ride* by David Hackett Fisher. Copyright © 1994 by Oxford University Press. Reprinted by permission of the publisher.

Back Bay Books/Little, Brown and Company
Hachette Book Group USA
237 Park Avenue
New York, NY 10017
Visit our Web site at www.HachetteBookGroupUSA.com

Printed in the United States of America

Originally published in hardcover by Little, Brown and Company
First Back Bay international paperback edition: May 2001

22 21 20 19 18 17 16 15

To my parents,
Joyce and Graham Gladwell

Contents

THE
TIPPING POINT

Introduction

For Hush Puppies — the classic American brushed-suede shoes with the lightweight crepe sole — the Tipping Point came somewhere between late 1994 and early 1995. The brand had been all but dead until that point. Sales were down to 30,000 pairs a year, mostly to backwoods outlets and small-town family stores. Wolverine, the company that makes Hush Puppies, was thinking of phasing out the shoes that made them famous. But then something strange happened. At a fashion shoot, two Hush Puppies executives — Owen Baxter and Geoffrey Lewis — ran into a stylist from New York who told them that the classic Hush Puppies had suddenly become hip in the clubs and bars of downtown Manhattan. "We were being told," Baxter recalls, "that there were resale shops in the Village, in Soho, where the shoes were being sold. People were going to the Ma and Pa stores, the little stores that still carried them, and buying them up." Baxter and Lewis were baffled at first. It made no sense to them that shoes that were so obviously out of fashion could make a comeback. "We were told that Isaac Mizrahi was wearing the shoes himself," Lewis says. "I think it's fair to say that at the time we had no idea who Isaac Mizrahi was."

By the fall of 1995, things began to happen in a rush. First the designer John Bartlett called. He wanted to use Hush Puppies in his spring collection. Then another Manhattan designer, Anna Sui, called, wanting shoes for her show as well. In Los Angeles, the designer Joel Fitzgerald put a twenty-five-foot inflatable basset hound — the symbol of the Hush Puppies brand — on the roof of his Hollywood store and gutted an adjoining art gallery to turn it into a Hush Puppies boutique. While he was still painting and putting up shelves, the actor Pee-wee Herman walked in and asked for a couple of pairs. "It was total word of mouth," Fitzgerald remembers.

In 1995, the company sold 430,000 pairs of the classic Hush Puppies, and the next year it sold four times that, and the year after that still more, until Hush Puppies were once again a staple of the wardrobe of the young American male. In 1996, Hush Puppies won the prize for best accessory at the Council of Fashion Designers awards dinner at Lincoln Center, and the president of the firm stood up on the stage with Calvin Klein and Donna Karan and accepted an award for an achievement that — as he would be the first to admit — his company had almost nothing to do with. Hush Puppies had suddenly exploded, and it all started with a handful of kids in the East Village and Soho.

How did that happen? Those first few kids, whoever they were, weren't deliberately trying to promote Hush

Puppies. They were wearing them precisely because no one else would wear them. Then the fad spread to two fashion designers who used the shoes to peddle something else — haute couture. The shoes were an incidental touch. No one was trying to make Hush Puppies a trend. Yet, somehow, that's exactly what happened. The shoes passed a certain point in popularity and they tipped. How does a thirty-dollar pair of shoes go from a handful of downtown Manhattan hipsters and designers to every mall in America in the space of two years?

1.

There was a time, not very long ago, in the desperately poor New York City neighborhoods of Brownsville and East New York, when the streets would turn into ghost towns at dusk. Ordinary working people wouldn't walk on the sidewalks. Children wouldn't ride their bicycles on the streets. Old folks wouldn't sit on stoops and park benches. The drug trade ran so rampant and gang warfare was so ubiquitous in that part of Brooklyn that most people would take to the safety of their apartment at nightfall. Police officers who served in Brownsville in the 1980s and early 1990s say that, in those years, as soon as the sun went down their radios exploded with chatter between beat officers and their dispatchers over every conceivable kind of violent and dangerous crime. In 1992, there were 2,154 murders in New York City and 626,182 serious crimes, with the weight of those crimes falling hardest in places like Brownsville and East New York. But then something strange happened. At some mysterious and critical point, the crime rate began to turn. It tipped. Within five years, murders had dropped 64.3 percent to 770 and total crimes had fallen by almost half to 355,893. In Brownsville and East New York, the sidewalks filled up again, the bicycles came back, and old folks reappeared on the stoops. "There was a time when it wasn't uncommon to hear rapid fire, like you would hear somewhere in the jungle in Vietnam," says Inspector Edward Messadri, who commands the police precinct in Brownsville. "I don't hear the gunfire anymore."

The New York City police will tell you that what happened in New York was that the city's policing strategies dramatically improved. Criminologists point to the decline of the crack trade and the aging of the population. Economists, meanwhile, say that the gradual improvement in the city's economy over the course of the 1990s had the effect of employing those who might otherwise have become criminals. These are the conventional explanations for the rise and fall of social problems, but in the end none is any more satisfying than the statement that kids in the East Village caused the Hush Puppies revival. The changes in the drug trade, the population, and the economy are all long-term trends, happening all over the country. They don't explain why crime plunged in New York City so much more than in other cities around the country, and they don't explain why it all happened in such an extraordinarily short time. As for the improvements made by the police, they are important too. But there is a puzzling gap between the scale of the changes in policing and the size of the effect on places like Brownsville and East New York. After all, crime didn't just slowly ebb in New York as conditions gradually improved. It plummeted. How can a change in a handful of economic and social indices cause murder rates to fall by two-thirds in five years?

2.

The Tipping Point is the biography of an idea, and the idea is very simple. It is that the best way to understand the emergence of fashion trends, the ebb and flow of crime waves, or, for that matter, the transformation of unknown books into bestsellers, or the rise of teenage smoking, or the phenomena of word of mouth, or any number of the other mysterious changes that mark everyday life is to think of them as epidemics. Ideas and products and messages and behaviors spread just like viruses do.

The rise of Hush Puppies and the fall of New York's crime rate are textbook examples of epidemics in action. Although they may sound as if they don't have very much in common, they share a basic, underlying pattern. First of all, they are clear examples of contagious behavior. No one took out an advertisement and told people that the traditional Hush Puppies were cool and they should start wearing them. Those kids simply wore the shoes when they went to clubs or cafes or walked the streets of downtown New York, and in so doing exposed other people to their fashion sense. They infected them with the Hush Puppies "virus."

The crime decline in New York surely happened the same way. It wasn't that some huge percentage of would-be murderers suddenly sat up in 1993 and decided not to commit any more crimes. Nor was it that the police managed magically to intervene in a huge percentage of situations that would otherwise have turned deadly. What happened is that the small number of people in the small number of situations in which the police or the new social forces had some impact started behaving very differently, and that behavior somehow spread to other would-be criminals in similar situations. Somehow a large number of people in New York got "infected" with an anti-crime virus in a short time.

The second distinguishing characteristic of these two examples is that in both cases little changes had big effects. All of the possible reasons for why New York's crime rate dropped are changes that happened at the margin; they were incremental changes. The crack trade leveled off. The population got a little older. The police force got a little better. Yet the effect was dramatic. So too with Hush Puppies. How many kids are we talking about who began wearing the shoes in downtown Manhattan? Twenty? Fifty? One hundred — at the most? Yet their actions seem to have single-handedly started an international fashion trend.

Finally, both changes happened in a hurry. They didn't build steadily and slowly. It is instructive to look at a chart of the crime rate in New York City from, say, the mid-1960s to the late 1990s. It looks like a giant arch. In 1965, there were 200,000 crimes in the city and from that point on the number begins a sharp rise, doubling in two years and continuing almost unbroken until it hits 650,000 crimes a year in the mid-1970s. It stays steady at that level for the next two decades, before plunging downward in 1992 as sharply as it rose thirty years earlier. Crime did not taper off. It didn't gently decelerate. It hit a certain point and jammed on the brakes.

These three characteristics — one, contagiousness; two, the fact that little causes can have big effects; and three, that change happens not gradually but at one dramatic moment — are the same three principles that define how measles moves through a grade-school classroom or the flu attacks every winter. Of the three, the third trait — the idea that epidemics can rise or fall in one dramatic moment — is the most important, because it is the principle that makes sense of the first two and that permits the greatest insight into why modern change happens the way it does. The name given to that one dramatic moment in an epidemic when everything can change all at once is the Tipping Point.

3.

A world that follows the rules of epidemics is a very different place from the world we think we live in now. Think, for a moment, about the concept of contagiousness. If I say that word to you, you think of colds and the flu or perhaps something very dangerous like HIV or Ebola. We have, in our minds, a very specific, biological notion of what contagiousness means. But if there can be epidemics of crime or epidemics of fashion, there must be all kinds of things just as contagious as viruses. Have you ever thought about yawning, for instance? Yawning is a surprisingly powerful act. Just because you read the word "yawning" in the previous two sentences — and the two additional "yawns" in this sentence — a good number of you will probably yawn within the next few minutes. Even as I'm writing this, I've yawned twice. If you're reading this in a public place, and you've just yawned, chances are that a good proportion of everyone who saw you yawn is now yawning too, and a good proportion of the people watching the people who watched you yawn are now yawning as well, and on and on, in an ever-widening, yawning circle.

Yawning is incredibly contagious. I made some of you reading this yawn simply by writing the word "yawn." The people who yawned when they saw you yawn, meanwhile, were infected by the sight of you yawning — which is a second kind of contagion. They might even have yawned if they only heard you yawn, because yawning is also aurally contagious: if you play an audiotape of a yawn to blind people, they'll yawn too. And finally, if you yawned as you read this, did the thought cross your mind — however unconsciously and fleetingly — that you might be tired? I suspect that for some of you it did, which means that yawns can also be emotionally contagious. Simply by writing the word, I can plant a feeling in your mind. Can the flu virus do that? Contagiousness, in other words, is an unexpected property of all kinds of things, and we have to remember that, if we are to recognize and diagnose epidemic change.

The second of the principles of epidemics — that little changes can somehow have big effects — is also a fairly radical notion. We are, as humans, heavily socialized to make a kind of rough approximation between cause and effect. If we want to communicate a strong emotion, if we want to convince someone that, say, we love them, we realize that we need to speak passionately and forthrightly. If we want to break bad news to someone, we lower our voices and choose our words carefully. We are trained to think that what goes into any transaction or relationship or system must be directly related, in intensity and dimension, to what comes out. Consider, for example, the following puzzle. I give you a large piece of paper, and I ask you to fold it over once, and then take that folded paper and fold it over again, and then again, and again, until you have refolded the original paper 50 times. How tall do you think the final stack is going to be? In answer to that question, most people will fold the sheet in their mind's eye, and guess that the pile would be as thick as a phone book or, if they're really courageous, they'll say that it would be as tall as a refrigerator. But the real answer is that the height of the stack would approximate the distance to the sun. And if you folded it over one more time, the stack would be as high as the distance to the sun and back. This is an example of what in mathematics is called a geometric progression. Epidemics are another example of geometric progression: when a virus spreads through a population, it doubles and doubles again, until it has (figuratively) grown from a single sheet of paper all the way to the sun in fifty steps. As human beings we have a hard time with this kind of progression, because the end result — the effect — seems far out of proportion to the cause. To appreciate the power of epidemics, we have to abandon this expectation about proportionality. We need to prepare ourselves for the possibility that sometimes big changes follow from small events, and that sometimes these changes can happen very quickly.

This possibility of sudden change is at the center of the idea of the Tipping Point and might well be the hardest of all to accept. The expression first came into popular use in the 1970s to describe the flight to the suburbs of whites living in the older cities of the American Northeast. When the number of incoming African Americans in a particular neighborhood reached a certain point — 20 percent, say — sociologists observed that the community would "tip": most of the remaining whites would leave almost immediately. The Tipping Point is the moment of critical mass, the threshold, the boiling point. There was a Tipping Point for violent crime in New York in the early 1990s, and a Tipping Point for the reemergence of Hush Puppies, just as there is a Tipping Point for the introduction of any new technology. Sharp introduced the first low-priced fax machine in 1984, and sold about 80,000 of those machines in the United States in that first year. For the next three years, businesses slowly and steadily bought more and more faxes, until, in 1987, enough people had faxes that it made sense for everyone to get a fax. Nineteen eighty-seven was the fax machine Tipping Point. A million machines were sold that year, and by 1989 two million new machines had gone into operation. Cellular phones have followed the same trajectory. Through the 1990s, they got smaller and cheaper, and service got better until 1998, when the technology hit a Tipping Point and suddenly everyone had a cell phone. (For an explanation of the mathematics of Tipping Points, see the Endnotes.)

All epidemics have Tipping Points. Jonathan Crane, a sociologist at the University of Illinois, has looked at the effect the number of role models in a community —

the professionals, managers, teachers whom the Census Bureau has defined as "high status" — has on the lives of teenagers in the same neighborhood. He found little difference in pregnancy rates or school drop-out rates in neighborhoods of between 40 and 5 percent of high-status workers. But when the number of professionals dropped below 5 percent, the problems exploded. For black schoolchildren, for example, as the percentage of high-status workers falls just 2.2 percentage points — from 5.6 percent to 3.4 percent — drop-out rates more than double. At the same Tipping Point, the rates of child-bearing for teenaged girls — which barely move at all up to that point — nearly double. We assume, intuitively, that neighborhoods and social problems decline in some kind of steady progression. But sometimes they may not decline steadily at all; at the Tipping Point, schools can lose control of their students, and family life can disintegrate all at once.

I remember once as a child seeing our family's puppy encounter snow for the first time. He was shocked and delighted and overwhelmed, wagging his tail nervously, sniffing about in this strange, fluffy substance, whimpering with the mystery of it all. It wasn't much colder on the morning of his first snowfall than it had been the evening before. It might have been 34 degrees the previous evening, and now it was 31 degrees. Almost nothing had changed, in other words, yet — and this was the amazing thing — everything had changed. Rain had become something entirely different. Snow! We are all, at heart, gradualists, our expectations set by the steady passage of time. But the world of the Tipping Point is a place where the unexpected becomes expected, where radical change is more than possibility. It is — contrary to all our expectations — a certainty.

In pursuit of this radical idea, I'm going to take you to Baltimore, to learn from the epidemic of syphilis in that city. I'm going to introduce three fascinating kinds of people I call Mavens, Connectors, and Salesmen, who play a critical role in the word-of-mouth epidemics that dictate our tastes and trends and fashions. I'll take you to the set of the children's shows *Sesame Street* and *Blue's Clues* and into the fascinating world of the man who helped to create the Columbia Record Club to look at how messages can be structured to have the maximum possible impact on all their audience. I'll take you to a high-tech company in Delaware to talk about the Tipping Points that govern group life and to the subways of New York City to understand how the crime epidemic was brought to an end there. The point of all of this is to answer two simple questions that lie at the heart of what we would all like to accomplish as educators, parents, marketers, business people, and policymakers. Why is it that some ideas or behaviors or products start epidemics and others don't? And what can we do to deliberately start and control positive epidemics of our own?

ONE

The Three Rules of Epidemics

I n the mid-1990s, the city of Baltimore was attacked by an epidemic of syphilis. In the space of a year, from 1995 to 1996, the number of children born with the disease increased by 500 percent. If you look at Baltimore's syphilis rates on a graph, the line runs straight for years and then, when it hits 1995, rises almost at a right angle.

What caused Baltimore's syphilis problem to tip? According to the Centers for Disease Control, the problem was crack cocaine. Crack is known to cause a dramatic increase in the kind of risky sexual behavior that leads to the spread of things like HIV and syphilis. It brings far more people into poor areas to buy drugs, which then increases the likelihood that they will take an infection home with them to their own neighborhood. It changes the patterns of social connections between neighborhoods. Crack, the CDC said, was the little push that the syphilis problem needed to turn into a raging epidemic.

John Zenilman of Johns Hopkins University in Balti-more, an expert on sexually transmitted diseases, has another explanation: the breakdown of medical services in the city's poorest neighborhoods. "In 1990–91, we had thirty-six thousand patient visits at the city's sexually transmitted disease clinics," Zenilman says. "Then the city decided to gradually cut back because of budgetary prob-lems. The number of clinicians [medical personnel] went from seventeen to ten. The number of physicians went from three to essentially nobody. Patient visits dropped to twenty-one thousand. There also was a similar drop in the amount of field outreach staff. There was a lot of politics — things that used to happen, like computer upgrades, didn't happen. It was a worst-case scenario of city bureaucracy not functioning. They would run out of drugs."

When there were 36,000 patient visits a year in the STD clinics of Baltimore's inner city, in other words, the disease was kept in equilibrium. At some point between 36,000 and 21,000 patient visits a year, according to Zenil-man, the disease erupted. It began spilling out of the inner city, up the streets and highways that connect those neigh-borhoods to the rest of the city. Suddenly, people who might have been infectious for a week before getting treated were now going around infecting others for two or three or four weeks before they got cured. The breakdown in treatment made syphilis a much bigger issue than it had been before.

There is a third theory, which belongs to John Pot-terat, one of the country's leading epidemiologists. His culprits are the physical changes in those years affecting

East and West Baltimore, the heavily depressed neighborhoods on either side of Baltimore's downtown, where the syphilis problem was centered. In the mid-1990s, he points out, the city of Baltimore embarked on a highly publicized policy of dynamiting the old 1960s-style public housing high-rises in East and West Baltimore. Two of the most publicized demolitions — Lexington Terrace in West Baltimore and Lafayette Courts in East Baltimore — were huge projects, housing hundreds of families, that served as centers for crime and infectious disease. At the same time, people began to move out of the old row houses in East and West Baltimore, as those began to deteriorate as well.

"It was absolutely striking," Potterat says, of the first time he toured East and West Baltimore. "Fifty percent of the row houses were boarded up, and there was also a process where they destroyed the projects. What happened was a kind of hollowing out. This fueled the diaspora. For years syphilis had been confined to a specific region of Baltimore, within highly confined sociosexual networks. The housing dislocation process served to move these people to other parts of Baltimore, and they took their syphilis and other behaviors with them."

What is interesting about these three explanations is that none of them is at all dramatic. The CDC thought that crack was the problem. But it wasn't as if crack came to Baltimore for the first time in 1995. It had been there for years. What they were saying is that there was a subtle increase in the severity of the crack problem in the mid-1990s, and that change was enough to set off the syphilis epidemic. Zenilman, likewise, wasn't saying that the STD clinics in Baltimore were shut down. They were simply scaled back, the number of clinicians cut from seventeen to ten. Nor was Potterat saying that all Baltimore was hollowed out. All it took, he said, was the demolition of a handful of housing projects and the abandonment of homes in key downtown neighborhoods to send syphilis over the top. It takes only the smallest of changes to shatter an epidemic's equilibrium.

The second, and perhaps more interesting, fact about these explanations is that all of them are describing a very different way of tipping an epidemic. The CDC is talking about the overall context for the disease — how the introduction and growth of an addictive drug can so change the environment of a city that it can cause a disease to tip. Zenilman is talking about the disease itself. When the clinics were cut back, syphilis was given a second life. It had been an acute infection. It was now a chronic infection. It had become a lingering problem that stayed around for weeks. Potterat, for his part, was focused on the people who were carrying syphilis. Syphilis, he was saying, was a disease carried by a certain kind of person in Baltimore — a very poor, probably drug-using, sexually active individual. If that kind of person was suddenly transported from his or her old neighborhood to a new one — to a new part of town, where syphilis had never been a problem before — the disease would have an opportunity to tip.

There is more than one way to tip an epidemic, in other words. Epidemics are a function of the people who transmit infectious agents, the infectious agent itself, and the environment in which the infectious agent is operating. And when an epidemic tips, when it is jolted out of equilibrium, it tips because something has happened, some change has occurred in one (or two or three) of those areas. These three agents of change I call the Law of the Few, the Stickiness Factor, and the Power of Context.

1.

When we say that a handful of East Village kids started the Hush Puppies epidemic, or that the scattering of the residents of a few housing projects was sufficient to start Baltimore's syphilis epidemic, what we are really saying is that in a given process or system some people matter more than others. This is not, on the face of it, a particularly radical notion. Economists often talk about the 80/20 Principle, which is the idea that in any situation roughly 80 percent of the "work" will be done by 20 percent of the participants. In most societies, 20 percent of criminals commit 80 percent of crimes. Twenty percent of motorists cause 80 percent of all accidents. Twenty percent of beer drinkers drink 80 percent of all beer. When it comes to epidemics, though, this disproportionality becomes even more extreme: a tiny percentage of people do the majority of the work.

Potterat, for example, once did an analysis of a gonorrhea epidemic in Colorado Springs, Colorado, looking at everyone who came to a public health clinic for treatment of the disease over the space of six months. He found that about half of all the cases came, essentially, from four neighborhoods representing about 6 percent of the geographic area of the city. Half of those in that 6 percent, in turn, were socializing in the same six bars. Potterat then interviewed 768 people in that tiny subgroup and found that 600 of them either didn't give gonorrhea to anyone else or gave it to only one other person. These people he called nontransmitters. The ones causing the epidemic to grow — the ones who were infecting two and three and four and five others with their disease — were the remaining 168. In other words, in all of the city of Colorado Springs — a town of well in excess of 100,000 people — the epidemic of gonorrhea tipped because of the activities of 168 people living in four small neighborhoods and basically frequenting the same six bars.

Who were those 168 people? They aren't like you or me. They are people who go out every night, people who have vastly more sexual partners than the norm, people whose lives and behavior are well outside of the ordinary. In the mid-1990s, for example, in the pool halls and roller-skating rinks of East St. Louis, Missouri, there was a man named Darnell "Boss Man" McGee. He was big — over six feet — and charming, a talented skater, who wowed young girls with his exploits on the rink. His specialty was thirteen- and fourteen-year-olds. He bought them jewelry, took them for rides in his Cadillac, got them high on crack, and had sex with them. Between 1995 and 1997, when he was shot dead by an unknown assailant, he slept with at least 100 women and — it turned out later — infected at least 30 of them with HIV.

In the same two-year period, fifteen hundred miles away, near Buffalo, New York, another man — a kind of Boss Man clone — worked the distressed downtown streets of Jamestown. His name was Nushawn Williams, although he also went by the names "Face," "Sly," and "Shyteek." Williams juggled dozens of girls, maintaining three or four different apartments around the city, and all the while supporting himself by smuggling drugs up from the Bronx. (As one epidemiologist familiar with the case told me flatly, "The man was a genius. If I could get away with what Williams did, I'd never have to work a day again in my life.") Williams, like Boss Man, was a charmer. He would buy his girlfriends roses, let them braid his long hair, and host all-night marijuana and malt liquor–fueled orgies at his apartments. "I slept with him three or four times in one night," one of his partners remembered. "Me and him, we used to party together all the time. . . . After Face had sex, his friends would do it too. One would walk out, the other would walk in." Williams is now in jail. He is known to have infected at least sixteen of his former girlfriends with the AIDS virus. And most famously, in the book *And the Band Played On* Randy Shilts discusses at length the so-called Patient Zero of AIDS, the French-Canadian flight attendant Gaetan Dugas, who claimed to have 2,500 sexual partners all over North America, and who was linked to at least 40 of the earliest cases of AIDS in California and New York. These are the kinds of people who make epidemics of disease tip.

Social epidemics work in exactly the same way. They are also driven by the efforts of a handful of exceptional people. In this case, it's not sexual appetites that set them apart. It's things like how sociable they are, or how energetic or knowledgeable or influential among their peers. In the case of Hush Puppies, the great mystery is how those shoes went from something worn by a few fashion-forward downtown Manhattan hipsters to being sold in malls across the country. What was the connection between the East Village and Middle America? The Law of the Few says the answer is that one of these exceptional people found out about the trend, and through social connections and energy and enthusiasm and personality spread the word about Hush Puppies just as people like Gaetan Dugas and Nushawn Williams were able to spread HIV.

2.

In Baltimore, when the city's public clinics suffered cutbacks, the nature of the syphilis affecting the city's poor neighborhoods changed. It used to be an acute infection, something that most people could get treated fairly quickly before they had a chance to infect many others. But with the cutbacks, syphilis increasingly became a chronic disease, and the disease's carriers had three or four or five times longer to pass on their infection. Epidemics tip because of the extraordinary efforts of a few select carriers. But they also sometimes tip when something happens to transform the epidemic agent itself.

This is a well-known principle in virology. The strains of flu that circulate at the beginning of each winter's flu epidemic are quite different from the strains of flu that circulate at the end. The most famous flu epidemic of all — the pandemic of 1918 — was first spotted in the spring of that year and was, relatively speaking, quite tame. But over the summer the virus underwent some strange transformation and over the next six months ended up killing between 20 and 40 million people worldwide. Nothing had changed in the way in which the virus was being spread. But the virus had suddenly become much more deadly.

The Dutch AIDS researcher Jaap Goudsmit argues that this same kind of dramatic transformation happened with HIV. Goudsmit's work focuses on what is known as *Pneumocystis carinii* pneumonia, or PCP. All of us carry the bacterium in our bodies, probably since birth or immediately thereafter. In most of us it is harmless. Our immune systems keep it in check easily. But if something, such as HIV, wipes out our immune system, it becomes so uncontrollable that it can cause a deadly form of pneumonia. PCP is so common among AIDS patients, in fact, that it has come to be seen as an almost certain indication of the presence of the virus. What Goudsmit did was go back in the medical literature and look for cases of PCP, and what he found is quite chilling. Just after World War II, beginning in the Baltic port city of Danzig and spreading through central Europe, there was an epidemic of PCP that claimed the lives of thousands of small children.

Goudsmit has analyzed one of the towns hit hardest by the PCP epidemic, the mining town of Heerlen in the Dutch province of Limburg. Heerlen had a training hospital for midwives called the Kweekschool voor Vroedvrouwen, a single unit of which — the so-called Swedish barrack — was used in the 1950s as a special ward for underweight or premature infants. Between June 1955 and July 1958, 81 infants in the Swedish barrack came down with PCP and 24 died. Goudsmit thinks that this was an early HIV epidemic, and that somehow the virus got into the hospital, and was spread from child to child by the then, apparently common, practice of using the same needles over and over again for blood transfusions or injections of antibiotics. He writes:

Most likely at least one adult — probably a coal miner from Poland, Czechoslovakia, or Italy — brought the virus to Limburg. This one adult could have died from AIDS with little notice. . . . He could have transmitted the virus to his wife and offspring. His infected wife (or girlfriend) could have given birth in a Swedish barrack to a child who was HIV infected but seemingly healthy. Unsterilized needles and syringes could have spread the virus from child to child.

The truly strange thing about this story, of course, is that not all of the children died. Only a third did. The others did what today would seem almost impossible. They defeated HIV, purged it from their bodies, and went on to live healthy lives. In other words, the strains of HIV that were circulating back in the 1950s were a lot different from the strains of HIV that circulate today. They were every bit as contagious. But they were weak enough that most people — even small children — were able to fight them off and survive them. The HIV epidemic tipped in the early 1980s, in short, not just because of the enormous changes in sexual behavior in the gay communities that made it possible for the virus to spread rapidly. It also tipped because HIV itself changed. For one reason or another, the virus became a lot deadlier. Once it infected you, you stayed infected. It stuck.

This idea of the importance of stickiness in tipping has enormous implications for the way we regard social epidemics as well. We tend to spend a lot of time thinking about how to make messages more contagious — how to reach as many people as possible with our products or ideas. But the hard part of communication is often figuring out how to make sure a message doesn't go in one ear and out the other. Stickiness means that a message makes an impact. You can't get it out of your head. It sticks in your memory. When Winston filter-tip cigarettes were introduced in the spring of 1954, for example, the company came up with the slogan "Winston tastes good like a cigarette should." At the time, the ungrammatical and somehow provocative use of "like" instead of "as" created a minor sensation. It was the kind of phrase that people talked about, like the famous Wendy's tag line from 1984 "Where's the beef?" In his history of the cigarette industry, Richard Kluger writes that the marketers at R. J. Reynolds, which sells Winston, were "delighted with the attention" and "made the offending slogan the lyric of a bouncy little jingle on television and radio, and wryly defended their syntax as a colloquialism rather than bad grammar." Within months of its introduction, on the strength of that catchy phrase, Winston tipped, racing past Parliament, Kent, and L&M into second place, behind Viceroy, in the American cigarette market. Within a few years, it was the bestselling brand in the country. To this day, if you say to most Americans "Winston tastes good," they can finish the phrase, "like a cigarette should." That's a classically sticky advertising line, and stickiness is a critical component in tipping. Unless you remember what I tell you, why would you ever change your behavior or buy my product or go to see my movie?

The Stickiness Factor says that there are specific ways of making a contagious message memorable; there are relatively simple changes in the presentation and structuring of information that can make a big difference in how much of an impact it makes.

3.

Every time someone in Baltimore comes to a public clinic for treatment of syphilis or gonorrhea, John Zenilman plugs his or her address into his computer, so that the case shows up as a little black star on a map of the city. It's rather like a medical version of the maps police departments put up on their walls, with pins marking where crimes have occurred. On Zenilman's map the neighborhoods of East and West Baltimore, on either side of the downtown core, tend to be thick with black stars. From those two spots, the cases radiate outward along the two central roadways that happen to cut through both neighborhoods. In the summer, when the incidence of sexually transmitted disease is highest, the clusters of black stars on the roads leading out of East and West Baltimore become thick with cases. The disease is on the move. But in the winter months, the map changes. When the weather turns cold, and the people of East and West Baltimore are much more likely to stay at home, away from the bars and clubs and street corners where sexual transactions are made, the stars in each neighborhood fade away.

The seasonal effect on the number of cases is so strong that it is not hard to imagine that a long, hard winter in Baltimore could be enough to slow or lessen substantially — at least for the season — the growth of the syphilis epidemic.

Epidemics, Zenilman's map demonstrates, are strongly influenced by their situation — by the circumstances and conditions and particulars of the environments in which they operate. This much is obvious. What is interesting, though, is how far this principle can be extended. It isn't just prosaic factors like the weather that influence behavior. Even the smallest and subtlest and most unexpected of factors can affect the way we act. One of the most infamous incidents in New York City history, for example, was the 1964 stabbing death of a young Queens woman by the name of Kitty Genovese. Genovese was chased by her assailant and attacked three times on the street, over the course of half an hour, as thirty-eight of her neighbors watched from their windows. During that time, however, none of the thirty-eight witnesses called the police. The case provoked rounds of self-recrimination. It became symbolic of the cold and dehumanizing effects of urban life. Abe Rosenthal, who would later become editor of the *New York Times,* wrote in a book about the case:

> Nobody can say why the thirty-eight did not lift the phone while Miss Genovese was being attacked, since they cannot say themselves. It can be assumed, however, that their apathy was indeed one of the big-city variety. It is almost a matter of psychological survival, if one is surrounded and pressed by millions of people, to prevent them from constantly impinging on you, and the only way to do this is to ignore them as often as possible. Indifference to one's neighbor and his troubles is a conditioned reflex in life in New York as it is in other big cities.

This is the kind of environmental explanation that makes intuitive sense to us. The anonymity and alienation of big-city life makes people hard and unfeeling. The truth about Genovese, however, turns out to be a little more complicated — and more interesting. Two New York City psychologists — Bibb Latane of Columbia University and John Darley of New York University — subsequently conducted a series of studies to try to understand what they dubbed the "bystander problem." They staged emergencies of one kind or another in different situations in order to see who would come and help. What they found, surprisingly, was that the one factor above all else that predicted helping behavior was how many witnesses there were to the event.

In one experiment, for example, Latane and Darley had a student alone in a room stage an epileptic fit. When there was just one person next door, listening, that person rushed to the student's aid 85 percent of the time. But when subjects thought that there were four others also overhearing the seizure, they came to the student's aid only 31 percent of the time. In another experiment, people who saw smoke seeping out from under a doorway would report it 75 percent of the time when they were on their own, but the incident would be reported only 38 percent of the time when they were in a group. When people are in a group, in other words, responsibility for acting is diffused. They assume that someone else will make the call, or they assume that because no one else is acting, the apparent problem — the seizure-like sounds from the other room, the smoke from the door — isn't really a problem. In the case of Kitty Genovese, then, social psychologists like Latane and Darley argue, the lesson is not that no one called despite the fact that thirty-eight people heard her scream; it's that no one called *because* thirty-eight people heard her scream. Ironically, had she been attacked on a lonely street with just one witness, she might have lived.

The key to getting people to change their behavior, in other words, to care about their neighbor in distress, sometimes lies with the smallest details of their immediate situation. The Power of Context says that human beings are a lot more sensitive to their environment than they may seem.

4.

The three rules of the Tipping Point — the Law of the Few, the Stickiness Factor, the Power of Context — offer a way of making sense of epidemics. They provide us with direction for how to go about reaching a Tipping Point. The balance of this book will take these ideas and apply them to other puzzling situations and epidemics from the world around us. How do these three rules help us understand teenage smoking, for example, or the phenomenon of word of mouth, or crime, or the rise of a bestseller? The answers may surprise you.

TWO

The Law of the Few

CONNECTORS, MAVENS, AND SALESMEN

O n the afternoon of April 18, 1775, a young boy who worked at a livery stable in Boston overheard one British army officer say to another something about "hell to pay tomorrow." The stable boy ran with the news to Boston's North End, to the home of a silversmith named Paul Revere. Revere listened gravely; this was not the first rumor to come his way that day. Earlier, he had been told of an unusual number of British officers gathered on Boston's Long Wharf, talking in low tones. British crewmen had been spotted scurrying about in the boats tethered beneath the HMS *Somerset* and the HMS *Boyne* in Boston Harbor. Several other sailors were seen on shore that morning, running what appeared to be last-minute errands. As the afternoon wore on, Revere and his close friend Joseph Warren became more and more convinced that the British were about to make the major move that had long been rumored — to march to the town of Lexington, northwest of Boston, to arrest the colonial leaders John Hancock and Samuel Adams, and then on to the town of Concord to seize the stores of guns and ammunition that some of the local colonial militia had stored there.

What happened next has become part of historical legend, a tale told to every American schoolchild. At ten o'clock that night, Warren and Revere met. They decided they had to warn the communities surrounding Boston that the British were on their way, so that local militia could be roused to meet them. Revere was spirited across Boston Harbor to the ferry landing at Charlestown. He jumped on a horse and began his "midnight ride" to Lexington. In two hours, he covered thirteen miles. In every town he passed through along the way — Charlestown, Medford, North Cambridge, Menotomy — he knocked on doors and spread the word, telling local colonial leaders of the oncoming British, and telling them to spread the word to others. Church bells started ringing. Drums started beating. The news spread like a virus as those informed by Paul Revere sent out riders of their own, until alarms were going off throughout the entire region. The word was in Lincoln, Massachusetts, by one A.M., in Sudbury by three, in Andover, forty miles northwest of Boston, by five A.M., and by nine in the morning had reached as far west as Ashby, near Worcester. When the British finally began their march toward Lexington on the morning of the nineteenth, their foray into the countryside was met — to their utter astonishment — with organized and fierce resistance. In Concord that day, the British were confronted and soundly beaten by the colonial militia, and from that exchange came the war known as the American Revolution.

Paul Revere's ride is perhaps the most famous historical example of a word-of-mouth epidemic. A piece of extraordinary news traveled a long distance in a very short time, mobilizing an entire region to arms. Not all word-of-mouth epidemics are this sensational, of course. But it is safe to say that word of mouth is — even in this age of mass communications and multimillion-dollar advertising campaigns — still the most important form of human communication. Think, for a moment, about the last expensive restaurant you went to, the last expensive piece of clothing you bought, and the last movie you saw. In how many of those cases was your decision about where to spend your money heavily influenced by the recommendation of a friend? There are plenty of advertising executives who think that precisely because of the sheer ubiquity of marketing efforts these days, word-of-mouth appeals have become the only kind of persuasion that most of us respond to anymore.

But for all that, word of mouth remains very mysterious. People pass on all kinds of information to each other all the time. But it's only in the rare instance that such an exchange ignites a word-of-mouth epidemic. There is a small restaurant in my neighborhood that I love and that I've been telling my friends about for six months. But it's still half empty. My endorsement clearly isn't enough to start a word-of-mouth epidemic, yet there are restaurants that to my mind aren't any better than the one in my neighborhood that open and within a matter of weeks are turning customers away. Why is it that some ideas and trends and messages "tip" and others don't?

In the case of Paul Revere's ride, the answer to this seems easy. Revere was carrying a sensational piece of news: the British were coming. But if you look closely at the events of that evening, that explanation doesn't solve the riddle either. At the same time that Revere began his ride north and west of Boston, a fellow revolutionary — a tanner by the name of William Dawes — set out on the same urgent errand, working his way to Lexington via the towns west of Boston. He was carrying the identical message, through just as many towns over just as many miles as Paul Revere. But Dawes's ride didn't set the countryside afire. The local militia leaders weren't alerted. In fact, so few men from one of the main towns he rode through — Waltham — fought the following day that some subsequent historians concluded that it must have been a strongly pro-British community. It wasn't. The people of Waltham just didn't find out the British were coming until it was too late. If it were only the news itself that mattered in a word-of-mouth epidemic, Dawes would now be as famous as Paul Revere. He isn't. So why did Revere succeed where Dawes failed?

The answer is that the success of any kind of social epidemic is heavily dependent on the involvement of people with a particular and rare set of social gifts. Revere's news tipped and Dawes's didn't because of the differences between the two men. This is the Law of the Few, which I briefly outlined in the previous chapter. But there I only gave examples of the kinds of people — highly promiscuous, sexually predatory — who are critical to epidemics of sexually transmitted disease. This chapter is about the people critical to social epidemics and what makes someone like Paul Revere different from someone like William Dawes. These kinds of people are all around us. Yet we often fail to give them proper credit for the role they play in our lives. I call them Connectors, Mavens, and Salesmen.

1.

In the late 1960s, the psychologist Stanley Milgram conducted an experiment to find an answer to what is known as the small-world problem. The problem is this: how are human beings connected? Do we all belong to separate worlds, operating simultaneously but autonomously, so that the links between any two people, anywhere in the world, are few and distant? Or are we all bound up together in a grand, interlocking web? In a way, Milgram was asking the very same kind of question that began this chapter, namely, how does an idea or a trend or a piece of news — the British are coming! — travel through a population?

Milgram's idea was to test this question with a chain letter. He got the names of 160 people who lived in Omaha, Nebraska, and mailed each of them a packet. In the packet was the name and address of a stockbroker who worked in Boston and lived in Sharon, Massachusetts. Each person was instructed to write his or her name on the packet and send it on to a friend or acquaintance who he or she thought would get the packet closer to the stockbroker. If you lived in Omaha and had a cousin outside of Boston, for example, you might send it to him, on the grounds that — even if your cousin did not himself know the stockbroker — he would be a lot more likely to be able to get to the stockbroker in two or three or four steps. The idea was that when the packet finally arrived at the stockbroker's house, Milgram could look at the list of all those whose hands it went through to get there and establish how closely connected someone chosen at random from one part of the country was to another person in another part of the country. Milgram found that most of the letters reached the stockbroker in five or six steps. This experiment is where we get the concept of six degrees of separation.

That phrase is now so familiar that it is easy to lose sight of how surprising Milgram's findings were. Most of us don't have particularly broad and diverse groups of friends. In one well-known study, a group of psychologists asked people living in the Dyckman public housing project in northern Manhattan to name their closest friend in the project; 88 percent of the friends lived in the same building, and half lived on the same floor. In general, people chose friends of similar age and race. But if the friend lived down the hall, then age and race became a lot less important. Proximity overpowered similarity. Another study, done on students at the University of Utah, found that if you ask someone why he is friendly with someone else, he'll say it is because he and his friend share similar attitudes. But if you actually quiz the two of them on their attitudes, you'll find out that what they actually share is similar activities. We're friends with the people we do things with, as much as we are with the people we resemble. We don't seek out friends, in other words. We associate with the people who occupy the same small, physical spaces that we do. People in Omaha are not, as a rule, friends with people who live halfway across the country in Sharon, Massachusetts. "When I asked an intelligent friend of mine how many steps he thought it would take, he estimated that it would require 100 intermediate persons or more to move from Nebraska to Sharon," Milgram wrote, at the time. "Many people make somewhat similar estimates, and are surprised to learn that only five intermediaries will — on average — suffice. Somehow it does not accord with intuition." How did the packet get to Sharon in just five steps?

The answer is that in the six degrees of separation, not all degrees are equal. When Milgram analyzed his experiment, for example, he found that many of the chains from Omaha to Sharon followed the same asymmetrical pattern. Twenty-four letters reached the stockbroker at his home in Sharon, and of those, sixteen were given to him by the same person, a clothing merchant Milgram calls Mr. Jacobs. The balance of letters came to the stockbroker at his office, and of those the majority came through two other men, whom Milgram calls Mr. Brown and Mr. Jones. In all, half of the responses that came back to the stockbroker were delivered to him by these same three people. Think of it. Dozens of people, chosen at random from a large Midwestern city, send out letters independently. Some go through college acquaintances. Some send their letters to relatives. Some send them to old workmates. Everyone has a different strategy. Yet in the end, when all of those separate and idiosyncratic chains were completed, half of those letters ended up in the hands of Jacobs, Jones, and Brown. Six degrees of separation doesn't mean that everyone is linked to everyone else in just six steps. It means that a very small number of people are linked to everyone else in a few steps, and the rest of us are linked to the world through those special few.

There is an easy way to explore this idea. Suppose that you made a list of the forty people whom you would call your circle of friends (not including family and co-workers) and in each case worked backward until you could identify the person who is ultimately responsible for setting in motion the series of connections that led to that friendship. My oldest friend, Bruce, for example, I met in first grade, so I'm the responsible party. That's easy. I met my friend Nigel because he lived down the hall in college from my friend Tom, whom I met because in freshman year he invited me to play touch football. Tom is responsible for Nigel. Once you've made all of the connections, the strange thing is that you will find the same names coming up again and again. I have a friend named Amy, whom I met when her friend Katie brought her to a restaurant where I was having dinner one night. I know Katie because she is the best friend of my friend Larissa, whom I know because I was told to look her up by a mutual friend of both of ours — Mike A. — whom I know because he went to school with another friend of mine — Mike H. — who used to work at a political weekly with my friend Jacob. No Jacob, no Amy. Similarly, I met my friend Sarah S. at my birthday party a year ago, because she was there with a writer named David who was there at the invitation of his agent, Tina, whom I met through my friend Leslie, whom I know because her sister, Nina, is a friend of my friend Ann's, whom I met through my old roommate Maura, who was my roommate because she worked with a writer named Sarah L., who was a college friend of my friend Jacob's. No Jacob, no Sarah S. In fact, when I go down my list of forty friends, thirty of them, in one way or another, lead back to Jacob. My social circle is, in reality, not a circle. It is a pyramid. And at the top of the pyramid is a single person — Jacob — who is responsible for an overwhelming majority of the relationships that constitute my life. Not only is my social circle not a circle, but it's not "mine" either. It belongs to Jacob. It's more like a club that he invited me to join. These people who link us up with the world, who bridge Omaha and Sharon, who introduce us to our social circles — these people on whom we rely more heavily than we realize — are Connectors, people with a special gift for bringing the world together.

2.

What makes someone a Connector? The first — and most obvious — criterion is that Connectors know lots of people. They are the kinds of people who know everyone. All of us know someone like this. But I don't think that we spend a lot of time thinking about the importance of these kinds of people. I'm not even sure that most of us really believe that the kind of person who knows everyone really knows everyone. But they do. There is a simple way to show this. In the paragraph below is a list of around 250 surnames, all taken at random from the Manhattan phone book. Go down the list and give yourself a point every time you see a surname that is shared by someone you know. (The definition of "know" here is very broad. For example, if you sat down next to that person on a train, you would know their name if they introduced themselves to you and they would know your name.) Multiple names count. If the name is Johnson, in other words, and you know three Johnsons, you get three points. The idea is that your score on this test should roughly represent how social you are. It's a simple way of estimating how many friends and acquaintances you have.

Algazi, Alvarez, Alpern, Ametrano, Andrews, Aran, Arnstein, Ashford, Bailey, Ballout, Bamberger, Baptista, Barr, Barrows, Baskerville, Bassiri, Bell, Bokgese, Brandao, Bravo, Brooke, Brightman, Billy, Blau, Bohen, Bohn, Borsuk, Brendle, Butler, Calle, Cantwell, Carrell, Chinlund, Cirker, Cohen, Collas, Couch, Callegher, Calcaterra, Cook, Carey, Cassell, Chen, Chung, Clarke, Cohn, Carton, Crowley, Curbelo, Dellamanna, Diaz, Dirar, Duncan, Dagostino, Delakas, Dillon, Donaghey, Daly, Dawson, Edery, Ellis, Elliott, Eastman, Easton, Famous, Fermin, Fialco, Finklestein, Farber, Falkin, Feinman, Friedman, Gardner, Gelpi, Glascock, Grandfield, Greenbaum, Greenwood, Gruber, Garil, Goff, Gladwell, Greenup, Gannon, Ganshaw, Garcia, Gennis, Gerard, Gericke, Gilbert, Glassman, Glazer, Gomendio, Gonzalez, Greenstein, Guglielmo, Gurman, Haberkorn, Hoskins, Hussein, Hamm, Hardwick, Harrell, Hauptman, Hawkins, Henderson, Hayman, Hibara, Hehmann, Herbst, Hedges, Hogan, Hoffman, Horowitz, Hsu, Huber, Ikiz, Jaroschy, Johann, Jacobs, Jara, Johnson, Kassel, Keegan, Kuroda, Kavanau, Keller, Kevill, Kiew, Kimbrough, Kline, Kossoff, Kotzitzky, Kahn, Kiesler,

Kosser, Korte, Leibowitz, Lin, Liu, Lowrance, Lundh, Laux, Leifer, Leung, Levine, Leiw, Lockwood, Logrono, Lohnes, Lowet, Laber, Leonardi, Marten, McLean, Michaels, Miranda, Moy, Marin, Muir, Murphy, Marodon, Matos, Mendoza, Muraki, Neck, Needham, Noboa, Null, O'Flynn, O'Neill, Orlowski, Perkins, Pieper, Pierre, Pons, Pruska, Paulino, Popper, Potter, Purpura, Palma, Perez, Portocarrero, Punwasi, Rader, Rankin, Ray, Reyes, Richardson, Ritter, Roos, Rose, Rosenfeld, Roth, Rutherford, Rustin, Ramos, Regan, Reisman, Renkert, Roberts, Rowan, Rene, Rosario, Rothbart, Saperstein, Schoenbrod, Schwed, Sears, Statosky, Sutphen, Sheehy, Silverton, Silverman, Silverstein, Sklar, Slotkin, Speros, Stollman, Sadowski, Schles, Shapiro, Sigdel, Snow, Spencer, Steinkol, Stewart, Stires, Stopnik, Stonehill, Tayss, Tilney, Temple, Torfield, Townsend, Trimpin, Turchin, Villa, Vasillov, Voda, Waring, Weber, Weinstein, Wang, Wegimont, Weed, Weishaus.

I have given this test to at least a dozen groups of people. One was a freshman World Civilizations class at City College in Manhattan. The students were all in their late teens or early twenties, many of them recent immigrants to America, and of middle and lower income. The average score in that class was 20.96, meaning that the average person in the class knew 21 people with the same last names as the people on my list. I also gave the test to a group of health educators and academics at a conference in Princeton, New Jersey. This group were mostly in their forties and fifties, largely white, highly educated — many had Ph.D.'s — and wealthy. Their average score was 39.

Then I gave the test to a relatively random sample of my friends and acquaintances, mostly journalists and professionals in their late twenties and thirties. The average score was 41. These results shouldn't be all that surprising. College students don't have as wide a circle of acquaintances as people in their forties. It makes sense that between the ages of twenty and forty the number of people you know should roughly double, and that upper-income professionals should know more people than lower-income immigrants. In every group there was also quite a range between the highest and the lowest scorers. That makes sense too, I think. Real estate salesmen know more people than computer hackers. What was surprising, though, was how enormous that range was. In the college class, the low score was 2 and the high score was 95. In my random sample, the low score was 9 and the high score was 118. Even at the conference in Princeton, which was a highly homogenous group of people of similar age, education, and income — who were all, with a few exceptions, in the same profession — the range was enormous. The lowest score was 16. The highest score was 108. All told, I have given the test to about 400 people. Of those, there were two dozen or so scores under 20, eight over 90, and four more over 100. The other surprising thing is that I found high scorers in every social group I looked at. The scores of the students at City College were less, on average, than adult scores. But even in that group there are people whose social circle is four or five times the size of other people's. Sprinkled among every walk of life, in other words, are a handful of people with a truly extraordinary knack of making friends and acquaintances. They are Connectors.

One of the highest scorers on my acquaintance survey was a man named Roger Horchow, who is a successful businessman from Dallas. Horchow founded the Horchow Collection, a high-end mail order merchandise company. He has also enjoyed considerable success on Broadway, backing such hits as *Les Miserables* and *Phantom of the Opera* and producing the award-winning Gershwin musical *Crazy for You.* I was introduced to Horchow through his daughter, who is a friend of mine, and I went to see him in his Manhattan pied-à-terre, an elegant apartment high above Fifth Avenue. Horchow is slender and composed. He talks slowly, with a slight Texas drawl. He has a kind of wry, ironic charm that is utterly winning. If you sat next to Roger Horchow on a plane ride across the Atlantic, he would start talking as the plane taxied to the runway, you would be laughing by the time the seatbelt sign was turned off, and when you landed at the other end you'd wonder where the time went. When I gave Horchow the list of names from the Manhattan directory, he went through the list very quickly, muttering names under his breath as his pencil skimmed the page. He scored 98. I suspect that had I given him another 10 minutes to think, he would have scored even higher.

Why did Horchow do so well? When I met him, I became convinced that knowing lots of people was a kind of skill, something that someone might set out to do deliberately and that could be perfected, and that those techniques were central to the fact that he knew everyone. I kept asking Horchow how all of the connections in his life had helped him in the business world, because I thought that the two things had to be linked, but the questions seemed to puzzle him. It wasn't that his connections hadn't helped him. It was that he didn't think of his people collection as a business strategy. He just thought of it as something he did. It was who he was. Horchow has an instinctive and natural gift for making social connections. He's not aggressive about it. He's not one of those overly social, back-slapping types for whom the process of acquiring acquaintances is obvious and self-serving. He's more an observer, with the dry, knowing manner of someone who likes to remain a little bit on the outside. He simply likes people, in a genuine and powerful way, and he finds the patterns of acquaintanceship and interaction in which people arrange themselves to be endlessly fascinating. When I met with Horchow, he explained to me how he won the rights to revive the Gershwin musical *Girl Crazy* as *Crazy for You*. The full story took twenty minutes. This is just a portion. If it seems at all calculating, it shouldn't. Horchow told this story with a gentle, self-mocking air. He was, I think, deliberately playing up the idiosyncrasies of his personality. But as a portrait of how his mind works — and of what makes someone a Connector — I think it's perfectly accurate:

I have a friend named Mickey Shannon, who lives in New York. He said, I know you love Gershwin. I have met George Gershwin's old girlfriend. Her name is Emily Paley. She was also the sister of Ira Gershwin's wife, Lenore. She lives in the Village and she has invited us to dinner. So anyway, I met Emily Paley, and I saw a picture Gershwin had painted of her. Her husband, Lou Paley, wrote with Ira Gershwin and George Gershwin early on, when Ira Gershwin still called himself Arthur Francis. That was one link. . . .

I had lunch with a fellow called Leopold Gadowsky, who is the son of Frances Gershwin, George Gershwin's sister. She married a composer named Gadowsky. Arthur Gershwin's son was also there. His name is Mark Gershwin. So they said — well, why should we let you have the rights to *Girl Crazy*? Who are you? You've never been in the theater. So then I started pulling out my coincidences. Your aunt, Emily Paley. I went to her house. The picture with her in the red shawl — you've seen that picture? I pulled out all the little links. Then we all went to Hollywood and we went over to Mrs. Gershwin's house and I said, I'm so happy to meet you. I knew your sister. I loved your husband's work. Oh, and then I pulled out my Los Angeles friend. When I was at Neiman Marcus, a lady wrote a cookbook. Her name was Mildred Knopf. Her husband was Edwin Knopf, the movie producer. He did Audrey Hepburn's stuff. His brother was the publisher. We introduced her cookbook in Dallas, and Mildred became a good friend. We just loved her, and when I was in L.A. I would call on her. I always keep up with people. Well, it turns out Edwin Knopf was George Gershwin's closest friend. They had Gershwin's pictures all over their house. He was with Gershwin when he wrote "Rhapsody in Blue" in Asheville, North Carolina. Mr. Knopf died. But Mildred's still living. She's ninety-eight now. So when I went to see Lee Gershwin, we mentioned that we had just been to see Mildred Knopf. She said — You know her? Oh, why haven't we met before? She gave us the rights immediately.

In the course of our conversation, Horchow did this over and again, delighting in tying together the loose ends of a lifetime. For his seventieth birthday, he attempted to track down a friend from elementary school named Bobby Hunsinger, whom he hadn't seen in sixty years. He sent letters to every Bobby Hunsinger he could find, asking them if they were the Hunsinger who lived at 4501 First Lane in Cincinnati.

This is not normal social behavior. It's a little unusual. Horchow collects people the same way others collect stamps. He remembers the boys he played with sixty years ago, the address of his best friend growing up, the name of the man his college girlfriend had a crush on when she spent her junior year overseas. These details are critical to Horchow. He keeps on his computer a roster of 1,600 names and addresses, and on each entry is a note describing the circumstances under which he met the person. When we were talking, he took out a little red pocket diary. "If I met you and like you and you happen to mention your birthday, I write it in and you'll get a birthday card from Roger Horchow. See here — Monday was Ginger Broom's birthday, and the Wittenbergs' first anniversary. And Alan Schwartz's birthday is Friday and our yard man's is Saturday."

Most of us, I think, shy away from this kind of cultivation of acquaintances. We have our circle of friends, to whom we are devoted. Acquaintances we keep at arm's length. The reason we don't send birthday cards to people we don't really care a great deal about is that we don't want to feel obliged to have dinner with them or see a movie with them or visit them when they're sick. The purpose of making an acquaintance, for most of us, is to evaluate whether we want to turn that person into a friend; we don't feel we have the time or the energy to maintain meaningful contact with everyone. Horchow is quite different. The people he puts in his diary or on his computer are acquaintances — people he might run into only once a year or once every few years — and he doesn't shy away from the obligation that that connection requires. He has mastered what sociologists call the "weak tie," a friendly yet casual social connection. More than that, he's happy with the weak tie. After I met Horchow, I felt slightly frustrated. I wanted to know him better, but I wondered whether I would ever have the chance. I don't think he shared the same frustration with me. I think he's someone who sees value and pleasure in a casual meeting.

Why is Horchow so different from the rest of us? He doesn't know. He thinks it has something to do with being an only child whose father was often away. But that doesn't really explain it. Perhaps it is best to call the Connector impulse simply that — an impulse, just one of the many personality traits that distinguish one human being from another.

3.

Connectors are important for more than simply the number of people they know. Their importance is also a function of the kinds of people they know. Perhaps the best way to understand this point is through the popular parlor game "Six Degrees of Kevin Bacon." The idea behind the game is to try to link any actor or actress, through the movies they've been in, to the actor Kevin Bacon in less than six steps. So, for example, O.J. Simpson was in *Naked Gun* with Priscilla Presley, who was in *Ford Fairlane* with Gilbert Gottfried, who was in *Beverly Hills Cop II* with Paul Reiser, who was in *Diner* with Kevin Bacon. That's four steps. Mary Pickford was in *Screen Snapshots* with Clark Gable, who was in *Combat America* with Tony Romano, who, thirty-five years later, was in *Starting Over* with Bacon. That's three steps. Recently, a computer scientist at the University of Virginia by the name of Brett Tjaden actually sat down and figured out what the average Bacon number is for the quarter million or so actors and actresses who have played in television films or major motion pictures and came up with 2.8312 steps. Anyone who has ever acted, in other words, can be linked to Bacon in an average of under three steps. That sounds impressive, except that Tjaden then went back and performed an even more heroic calculation, figuring out what the average degree of connectedness was for everyone who had ever acted in Hollywood. For example, how many steps on average does it take to link everyone in Hollywood to Robert DeNiro or Shirley Temple or Adam Sandler? Tjaden found that when he listed all Hollywood actors in order of their "connectedness," Bacon ranked only 669th. Martin Sheen, by contrast, can be connected to every other actor in 2.63681 steps, which puts him almost 650 places higher than Bacon. Elliot Gould can be connected even more quickly, in 2.63601. Among the top fifteen are people like Robert Mitchum and Gene Hackman and Donald Sutherland and Shelley Winters and Burgess Meredith. The best-connected actor of all time? Rod Steiger.

Why is Kevin Bacon so far behind these actors? One big factor is that Bacon is a lot younger than most of them and as a result has made fewer movies. But that explains only some of the difference. There are lots of people, for example, who have made lots of movies and aren't particularly well connected. John Wayne, for example, made an extraordinary 179 movies in his sixty-year career and still ranks only 116th, at 2.7173. The problem is that more than half of John Wayne's movies were Westerns, meaning that he made the same kind of movie with the same kind of actors over and over again.

But take someone like Steiger: he has made great movies like the Oscar-winning *On the Waterfront* and dreadful movies like *Car Pool.* He won an Oscar for his role in *In the Heat of the Night* and also made "B" movies so bad they went straight to video. He's played Mussolini, Napoléon, Pontius Pilate, and Al Capone. He's been in thirty-eight dramas, twelve crime pictures and comedies, eleven thrillers, eight action films, seven Westerns, six war movies, four documentaries, three horror flicks, two sci-fi films, and a musical, among others. Rod Steiger is the best-connected actor in history because he has managed to move up and down and back and forth among all the different worlds and subcultures and niches and levels that the acting profession has to offer.

This is what Connectors are like. They are the Rod Steigers of everyday life. They are people whom all of us can reach in only a few steps because, for one reason or another, they manage to occupy many different worlds and subcultures and niches. In Steiger's case, of course, his high connectedness is a function of his versatility as an actor and, in all likelihood, some degree of good luck. But in the case of Connectors, their ability to span many different worlds is a function of something intrinsic to their personality, some combination of curiosity, self-confidence, sociability, and energy.

I once met a classic Connector in Chicago by the name of Lois Weisberg. Weisberg serves as the Commissioner of Cultural Affairs for the City of Chicago. But that is only the latest in what has been an extraordinary string of experiences and careers. In the early 1950s, for example, Weisberg ran a drama troupe in Chicago. In 1956, she decided to stage a festival to mark the centenary of George Bernard Shaw's birth, and then began putting out a newspaper devoted to Shaw, which mutated into an underground, alternative weekly called *The Paper*. On Friday nights people from all over the city would gather there for editorial meetings. William Friedkin, who would go on to direct *The French Connection* and *The Exorcist*, was a regular, as was the attorney Elmer Gertz (who was one of Nathan Leopold's attorneys) and some of the editors from *Playboy*, which was just up the street. People like Art Farmer and Thelonius Monk and John Coltrane and Lenny Bruce would stop by when they were in town. (Bruce actually lived with Weisberg for a while. "My mother was hysterical about it, especially one day when she rang the doorbell and he answered in a bath towel," Weisberg says. "We had a window on the porch, and he didn't have a key, so the window was always left open for him. There were a lot of rooms in that house, and a lot of people stayed there and I didn't know they were there. I never could stand his jokes. I didn't really like his act. I couldn't stand all the words he was using.") After *The Paper* folded, Lois took a job doing public relations for an injury rehabilitation institute. From there, she went to work for a public interest law firm called BPI, and while at BPI she became obsessed with the fact that Chicago's parks were crumbling and neglected, so she gathered together a motley collection of nature lovers, historians, civic activists, and housewives and founded a lobbying group called Friends of the Parks. Then she became alarmed because a commuter railroad that ran along the south shore of Lake Michigan — from South Bend to Chicago — was about to shut down, so she gathered together a motley collection of railway enthusiasts, environmentalists, and commuters and founded South Shore Recreation, and saved the railroad. Then she became executive director of the Chicago Council of Lawyers, a progressive legal group. Then she ran a local congressman's campaign. Then she got the position of director of special events for the first black mayor of Chicago, Harold Washington. Then she quit government and opened a small stand in a flea market. Then she went to work for Mayor Richard Daley — where she is to this day — as Chicago's Commissioner of Cultural Affairs.

If you go through that history and keep count, the number of worlds that Lois has belonged to comes to eight: the actors, the writers, the doctors, the lawyers, the park-lovers, the politicians, the railroad buffs, and the flea market aficionados. When I asked Weisberg to make her own list, she came up with ten, because she added the architects and the hospitality industry people she works with in her current job. But she was probably being modest, because if you looked harder at Weisberg's life you could probably subdivide her experiences into fifteen or twenty worlds. They aren't separate worlds, though. The point about Connectors is that by having a foot in so many different worlds, they have the effect of bringing them all together.

Once — and this would have been in the mid-1950s — Weisberg took the train to New York to attend, on a whim, the Science Fiction Writers Convention, where she met a young writer by the name of Arthur C. Clarke. Clarke took a shine to Weisberg, and next time he was in Chicago he called her up. "He was at a pay phone," Weisberg recalls. "He said, is there anyone in Chicago I should meet. I told him to come over to my house." Weisberg has a low, raspy voice, baked hard by half a century of nicotine, and she pauses between sentences to give herself the opportunity for a quick puff. Even when she's not smoking, she pauses anyway, as if to keep in practice for those moments when she is. "I called Bob Hughes. Bob Hughes was one of the people who wrote for my paper." Pause. "I said, do you know anyone in Chicago interested in talking to Arthur Clarke. He said, yeah, Isaac Asimov is in town. And this guy Robert, Robert — Robert Heinlein. So they all came over and sat in my study." Pause. "Then they called over to me and they said, Lois . . . I can't remember the word they used. They had some word for me. It was something about how I was the kind of person who brings people together."

This is in some ways the archetypal Lois Weisberg story. First she reaches out to somebody, to someone outside her world. She was in drama at the time. Arthur Clarke wrote science fiction. Then, equally important, that person responds to her. Lots of us reach out to those different from ourselves, or to those more famous or successful than we are, but that gesture isn't always reciprocated. Then there's the fact that when Arthur Clarke comes to Chicago and wants to be connected, to be linked up with someone else, Weisberg comes up with Isaac Asimov. She says it was a fluke that Asimov was in town. But if it wasn't Asimov, it would have been someone else.

One of the things that people remember about Weisberg's Friday night salons back in the 1950s was that they were always, effortlessly, racially integrated. The point is not that without that salon blacks wouldn't have socialized with whites on the North Side. It was rare back then, but it happened. The point is that when blacks socialized with whites in the 1950s in Chicago, it didn't happen by accident; it happened because a certain kind of person made it happen. That's what Asimov and Clarke meant when they said that Weisberg has this thing — whatever it is — that brings people together.

"She doesn't have any kind of snobbery," says Wendy Willrich, who used to work for Weisberg. "I once went with her on a trip to someone's professional photography studio. People write her letters and she looks at all of her mail, and the guy who owned the studio invited her out and she said yes. He was basically a wedding photographer. She decided to check it out. I was thinking, ohmigod, do we have to hike out forty-five minutes to this studio? It was out by the airport. This is the Commissioner of Cultural Affairs for the City of Chicago we're talking about. But she thought he was incredibly interesting." Was he actually interesting? Who knows? The point is that Lois found him interesting, because, in some way, she finds everyone interesting. Weisberg, one of her friends told me, "always says — 'Oh, I've met the most wonderful person. You are going to love her,' and she is as enthused about this person as she was about the first person she has met and you know what, she's usually right." Helen Doria, another of her friends, told me that "Lois sees things in you that you don't even see in yourself," which is another way of saying the same thing, that by some marvelous quirk of nature, Lois and the other people like her have some instinct that helps them relate to the people they meet. When Weisberg looks out at the world or when Roger Horchow sits next to you on an airplane, they don't see the same world that the rest of us see. They see possibility, and while most of us are busily choosing whom we would like to know, and rejecting the people who don't look right or who live out near the airport, or whom we haven't seen in sixty-five years, Lois and Roger like them all.

4.

There is a very good example of the way Connectors function in the work of the sociologist Mark Granovetter. In his classic 1974 study *Getting a Job*, Granovetter looked at several hundred professional and technical workers from the Boston suburb of Newton, interviewing them in some detail on their employment history. He found that

56 percent of those he talked to found their job through a personal connection. Another 18.8 percent used formal means — advertisements, headhunters — and roughly 20 percent applied directly. This much is not surprising; the best way to get in the door is through a personal contact. But, curiously, Granovetter found that of those personal connections, the majority were "weak ties." Of those who used a contact to find a job, only 16.7 percent saw that contact "often" — as they would if the contact were a good friend — and 55.6 percent saw their contact only "occasionally." Twenty-eight percent saw the contact "rarely." People weren't getting their jobs through their friends. They were getting them through their acquaintances.

Why is this? Granovetter argues that it is because when it comes to finding out about new jobs — or, for that matter, new information, or new ideas — "weak ties" are always more important than strong ties. Your friends, after all, occupy the same world that you do. They might work with you, or live near you, and go to the same churches, schools, or parties. How much, then, would they know that you wouldn't know? Your acquaintances, on the other hand, by definition occupy a very different world than you. They are much more likely to know something that you don't. To capture this apparent paradox, Granovetter coined a marvelous phrase: the strength of weak ties. Acquaintances, in short, represent a source of social power, and the more acquaintances you have the more powerful you are. Connectors like Lois Weisberg and Roger Horchow — who are masters of the weak tie — are extraordinarily powerful. We rely on them to give us access to opportunities and worlds to which we don't belong.

This principle holds for more than just jobs, of course. It also holds for restaurants, movies, fashion trends, or anything else that moves by word of mouth. It isn't just the case that the closer someone is to a Connector, the more powerful or the wealthier or the more opportunities he or she gets. It's also the case that the closer an idea or a product comes to a Connector, the more power and opportunity it has as well. Could this be one of the reasons Hush Puppies suddenly became a major fashion trend? Along the way from the East Village to Middle America, a Connector or a series of Connectors must have suddenly become enamored of them, and through their enormous social connections, their long lists of weak ties, their role in multiple worlds and subcultures, they must have been able to take those shoes and send them in a thousand directions at once — to make them really tip. Hush Puppies, in a sense then, got lucky. And perhaps one of the reasons why so many fashion trends don't make it into mainstream America is that simply, by sheerest bad fortune, they never happen to meet the approval of a Connector along the way.

Horchow's daughter, Sally, told me a story of how she once took her father to a new Japanese restaurant where a friend of hers was a chef. Horchow liked the food, and so when he went home he turned on his computer, pulled up the names of acquaintances who lived nearby, and faxed them notes telling them of a wonderful new restaurant he had discovered and that they should try it. This is, in a nutshell, what word of mouth is. It's not me telling you about a new restaurant with great food, and you telling a friend and that friend telling a friend. Word of mouth begins when somewhere along that chain, someone tells a person like Roger Horchow.

5.

Here, then, is the explanation for why Paul Revere's midnight ride started a word-of-mouth epidemic and William Dawes's ride did not. Paul Revere was the Roger Horchow or the Lois Weisberg of his day. He was a Connector. He was, for example, gregarious and intensely social. When he died, his funeral was attended, in the words of one contemporary newspaper account, by "troops of people." He was a fisherman and a hunter, a cardplayer and a theater-lover, a frequenter of pubs and a successful businessman. He was active in the local Masonic Lodge and was a member of several select social clubs. He was also a doer, a man blessed — as David Hackett Fischer recounts in his brilliant book *Paul Revere's Ride* — with an "uncanny genius for being at the center of events." Fischer writes:

> When Boston imported its first streetlights in 1774, Paul Revere was asked to serve on the committee that made the arrangement. When the Boston market required regulation, Paul Revere was appointed its clerk. After the Revolution, in a time of epidemics, he was chosen health officer of Boston, and coroner of Suffolk County. When a major fire ravaged the old wooden town, he helped to found the Massachusetts Mutual Fire Insurance Company, and his name was first to appear on its charter of incorporation. As poverty became a growing problem in the new republic, he called the meeting that organized the Massachusetts Charitable Mechanic Association, and

was elected its first president. When the community of Boston was shattered by the most sensational murder trial of his generation, Paul Revere was chosen foreman of the jury.

Had Revere been given a list of 250 surnames drawn at random from the Boston census of 1775, there is no question he would have scored well over 100.

After the Boston Tea Party, in 1773, when the anger of the American colonists against their British rulers began to spill over, dozens of committees and congresses of angry colonists sprang up around New England. They had no formal organization or established means of community. But Paul Revere quickly emerged as a link between all those far-flung revolutionary dots. He would routinely ride down to Philadelphia or New York or up to New Hampshire, carrying messages from one group to another. Within Boston as well, he played a special role. There were, in the revolutionary years, seven groups of "Whigs" (revolutionaries) in Boston, comprising some 255 men. Most of the men — over 80 percent — belonged to just one group. No one was a member of all seven. Only two men were members of as many as five of the groups: Paul Revere was one of those two.

It is not surprising, then, that when the British army began its secret campaign in 1774 to root out and destroy the stores of arms and ammunition held by the fledgling revolutionary movement, Revere became a kind of unofficial clearing house for the anti-British forces. He knew everybody. He was the logical one to go to if you were a stable boy on the afternoon of April 18th, 1775, and overheard two British officers talking about how there would be hell to pay on the following afternoon. Nor is it surprising that when Revere set out for Lexington that night, he would have known just how to spread the news as far and wide as possible. When he saw people on the roads, he was so naturally and irrepressibly social he would have stopped and told them. When he came upon a town, he would have known exactly whose door to knock on, who the local militia leader was, who the key players in town were. He had met most of them before. And they knew and respected him as well.

But William Dawes? Fischer finds it inconceivable that Dawes could have ridden all seventeen miles to Lexington and not spoken to anyone along the way. But he clearly had none of the social gifts of Revere, because there is almost no record of anyone who remembers him that night. "Along Paul Revere's northern route, the town leaders and company captains instantly triggered the alarm," Fischer writes. "On the southerly circuit of William Dawes, that did not happen until later. In at least one town it did not happen at all. Dawes did not awaken the town fathers or militia commanders in the towns of Roxbury, Brookline, Watertown, or Waltham." Why? Because Roxbury, Brookline, Watertown, and Waltham were not Boston. And Dawes was in all likelihood a man with a normal social circle, which means that — like most of us — once he left his hometown he probably wouldn't have known whose door to knock on. Only one small community along Dawes's ride appeared to get the message, a few farmers in a neighborhood called Waltham Farms. But alerting just those few houses wasn't enough to tip the alarm. Word-of-mouth epidemics are the work of Connectors. William Dawes was just an ordinary man.

6.

It would be a mistake, however, to think that Connectors are the only people who matter in a social epidemic. Roger Horchow sent out a dozen faxes promoting his daughter's friend's new restaurant. But he didn't discover that restaurant. Someone else did and told him about it. At some point in the rise of Hush Puppies, the shoes were discovered by Connectors, who broadcast the return of Hush Puppies far and wide. But who told the Connectors about Hush Puppies? It's possible that Connectors learn about new information by an entirely random process, that because they know so many people they get access to new things wherever they pop up. If you look closely at social epidemics, however, it becomes clear that just as there are people we rely upon to connect us to other people, there are also people we rely upon to connect us with new information. There are people specialists, and there are information specialists.

Sometimes, of course, these two specialties are one and the same. Part of the particular power of Paul Revere, for example, was that he wasn't just a networker; he wasn't just the man with the biggest Rolodex in colonial Boston. He was also actively engaged in gathering information about the British. In the fall of 1774, he set up a secret group that met regularly at the Green Dragon Tavern with the express purpose of monitoring British troop movements. In December of that year, the group learned that the British intended to seize a cache of ammunition being stored by a colonial militia near the entrance to Portsmouth Harbor, fifty miles north of Boston. On the icy morning of December 13th, Revere rode north through deep snow to warn the local militia that the British were on their way. He helped find out the intelligence, and he passed it on. Paul Revere was a Connector. But he was also — and this is the second of the three kinds of people who control word-of-mouth epidemics — a Maven.

The word *Maven* comes from the Yiddish, and it means one who accumulates knowledge. In recent years, economists have spent a great deal of time studying Mavens, for the obvious reason that if marketplaces depend on information, the people with the most information must be the most important. For example, sometimes when a supermarket wants to increase sales of a given product, they'll put a promotion sticker in front of it, saying something like "Everyday Low Price!" The price will stay the same. The product will just be featured more prominently. When they do that, supermarkets find that invariably the sales of the product will go through the roof, the same way they would if the product had actually been put on sale.

This is, when you think about it, a potentially disturbing piece of information. The whole premise behind sales, or supermarket specials, is that we, as consumers, are very aware of the prices of things and will react accordingly: we buy more in response to lower prices and less in response to higher prices. But if we'll buy more of something even if the price hasn't been lowered, then what's to stop supermarkets from never lowering their prices? What's to stop them from cheating us with meaningless "everyday low price" signs every time we walk in? The answer is that although most of us don't look at prices, every retailer knows that a very small number of people do, and if they find something amiss — a promotion that's not really a promotion — they'll do something about it. If a store tried to pull the sales stunt too often, these are the people who would figure it out and complain to management and tell their friends and acquaintances to avoid the store. These are the people who keep the marketplace honest. In the ten years or so since this group was first identified, economists have gone to great lengths to understand them. They have found them in every walk of life and in every socioeconomic group. One name for them is "price vigilantes." The other, more common, name for them is "Market Mavens."

Linda Price, a marketing professor at the University of Nebraska and a pioneer in Maven research, has made videotapes of interviews she's done with a number of Mavens. In one, a very well dressed man talks with great animation about how he goes about shopping. Here is the segment, in full:

> Because I follow the financial pages closely, I start to see trends. A classic example is with coffee. When the first coffee crunch came ten years ago, I had been following the thing about Brazilian frost and what it would do to the long-term price of coffee, and so I said I'm going to stockpile coffee.

At this point in the interview, an enormous smile breaks across the man's face.

I ended up with probably somewhere between thirty-five and forty cans of coffee. And I got them at these ridiculous prices, when the three-pound cans were $2.79 and $2.89. . . . Today it's about $6 for a three-pound can. I had fun doing that.

Do you see the level of obsession here? He can remember prices, to the cents, of cans of coffee he bought ten years ago.

The critical thing about Mavens, though, is that they aren't passive collectors of information. It isn't just that they are obsessed with how to get the best deal on a can of coffee. What sets them apart is that once they figure out how to get that deal, they want to tell you about it too. "A Maven is a person who has information on a lot of different products or prices or places. This person likes to initiate discussions with consumers and respond to requests," Price says. "They like to be helpers in the marketplace. They distribute coupons. They take you shopping. They go shopping for you. . . . They distribute about four times as many coupons as other people. This is the person who connects people to the marketplace and has the inside scoop on the marketplace. They know where the bathroom is in retail stores. That's the kind of knowledge they have." They are more than experts. An expert, says Price, will "talk about, say, cars because they love cars. But they don't talk about cars because they love you, and want to help you with your decision. The Market Maven will. They are more socially motivated."

Price says that well over half of Americans know a Maven, or someone close to the Maven's description. She herself, in fact, based the concept around someone she met when she was in graduate school, a man so memorable that his personality serves as the basis for what is now an entire field of research in the marketing world.

"I was doing my Ph.D. at the University of Texas," Price said. "At the time I didn't realize it, but I met the perfect Maven. He's Jewish and it was Easter and I was looking for a ham and I asked him. And he said, well, you know I am Jewish, but here's the deli you should go to and here's the price you should pay." Price started laughing at the memory. "You should look him up. His name is Mark Alpert."

7.

Mark Alpert is a slender, energetic man in his fifties. He has dark hair and a prominent nose and two small, burning, intelligent eyes. He talks quickly and precisely and with absolute authority. He's the kind of person who doesn't say that it was hot yesterday. He would say that we had a high of 87 degrees yesterday. He doesn't walk up stairs. He runs up them, like a small boy. He gives the sense that he is interested in and curious about everything, that, even at his age, if you gave him a children's chemistry set he would happily sit down right then and there and create some strange new concoction.

Alpert grew up in the Midwest, the son of a man who ran the first discount store in northern Minnesota. He got his doctorate from the University of Southern California and now teaches at the University of Texas School of Business Administration. But there is really no connection between his status as an economist and his Mavenism. Were Alpert a plumber, he would be just as exacting and thorough and knowledgeable about the ways of the marketplace.

We met over lunch at a restaurant on the lakefront in Austin. I got there first and chose a table. He got there second and persuaded me to move to another table, which he said was better. It was. I asked him about how he buys whatever he buys, and he began to talk. He explained why he has cable TV, as opposed to a dish. He gave me the inside scoop on Leonard Maltin's new movie guide. He gave me the name of a contact at the Park Central Hotel in Manhattan who is very helpful in getting a great deal. ("Malcolm, the hotel is ninety-nine dollars. And the rack rate is a hundred and eighty-nine dollars!") He explained what a rack rate is. (The initial, but soft, retail asking price for a hotel room.) He pointed at my tape recorder. "I think your tape is finished," he said. It was. He explained why I should not buy an Audi. ("They're Germans, so it's a pain dealing with them. For a while they would give you an under-the-counter warranty, but they don't anymore. The dealer network is small, so it's hard to get service. I love driving them. I don't like owning them." What I should drive, he told me, is a Mercury Mystique because they drive like a much more expensive European sedan. "They aren't selling well, so you can get a good deal. You go to a fleet buyer. You go in on the twenty-fifth of the month. You know this . . .") Then he launched into an impossibly long, sometimes hilarious, description of the several months he took to buy a new TV. If you or I had gone through the same experience — which involved sending televisions back, and laborious comparison of the tiniest electronic details and warranty fine print — I suspect we would have found it hellish. Alpert, apparently, found it exhilarating. Mavens, according to Price, are the kinds of people who are avid readers of *Consumer Reports*. Alpert is the kind of Maven who writes to *Consumer Reports* to correct them. "One time they said that the Audi 4000 was based on the Volkswagen Dasher. This was the late 1970s. But the Audi 4000 is a bigger car. I wrote them a letter. Then there was the Audi 5000 fiasco. *Consumer Reports* put them on their list of thou shalt not buy because of this sudden acceleration problem. But I read up on the problem in the literature and came to believe it was bogus. . . . So I wrote them and I said, you really ought to look into this. I gave them some information to consider. But I didn't hear back from them. It annoyed the hell out of me. They are supposed to be beyond that." He shook his head in disgust. He had out-Mavened the Maven bible.

Alpert is not, it should be said, an obnoxious know-it-all. It's easy to see how he could be, of course. Even Alpert is aware of that. "I was standing next to a kid in the supermarket who had to show his I.D. to buy cigarettes," Alpert told me. "I was very tempted to tell him I was diagnosed with lung cancer. In a way, that desire to be of service and influence — whatever it is — can be taken too far. You can become nosy. I try to be a very passive Maven. . . . You have to remember that it's their decision. It's their life." What saves him is that you never get the sense that he's showing off. There's something automatic, reflexive, about his level of involvement in the marketplace. It's not an act. It's very similar to the social instinct of Horchow and

Weisberg. At one point Alpert launched into a complicated story of how to make the best use of coupons in renting videos at Blockbuster. Then he stopped himself, as if he realized what he was saying, and burst out laughing. "Look, you can save a whole dollar! In a year's time I could probably save enough for a whole bottle of wine." Alpert is almost pathologically helpful. He can't help himself. "A Maven is someone who wants to solve other people's problems, generally by solving his own," Alpert said, which is true, although what I suspect is that the opposite is also true, that a Maven is someone who solves his own problems — his own emotional needs — by solving other people's problems. Something in Alpert was fulfilled in knowing that I would thereafter buy a television or a car or rent a hotel room in New York armed with the knowledge he had given me.

"Mark Alpert is a wonderfully unselfish man," Leigh MacAllister, a colleague of his at the University of Texas, told me. "I would say he saved me fifteen thousand dollars when I first came to Austin. He helped me negotiate the purchase of a house, because he understands the real estate game. I needed to get a washer and dryer. He got me a deal. I needed to get a car. I wanted to get a Volvo because I wanted to be just like Mark. Then he showed me an on-line service that had the prices of Volvos all over the State of Texas and went with me to buy the car. He helped me through the maze of all the retirement plans at the University of Texas. He simplified everything. He has everything processed. That's Mark Alpert. That's a Market Maven. God bless him. He's what makes the American system great."

8.

What makes people like Mark Alpert so important in starting epidemics? Obviously they know things that the rest of us don't. They read more magazines than the rest of us, more newspapers, and they may be the only people who read junk mail. Mark Alpert happens to be a connoisseur of electronic equipment. If there was a breakthrough new television or videocamera, and you were a friend of his, you can bet you would hear all about it quickly. Mavens have the knowledge and the social skills to start word-of-mouth epidemics. What sets Mavens apart, though, is not so much what they know but how they pass it along. The fact that Mavens want to help, for no other reason than because they like to help, turns out to be an awfully effective way of getting someone's attention.

This is surely part of the explanation for why Paul Revere's message was so powerful on the night of his midnight ride. News of the British march did not come by fax, or by means of a group e-mail. It wasn't broadcast on the nightly news, surrounded by commercials. It was carried by a man, a volunteer, riding on a cold night with no personal agenda other than a concern for the liberty of his peers. With Hush Puppies as well, perhaps the shoes caught the attention of Connectors precisely because they weren't part of any self-conscious, commercial fashion trend. Maybe a fashion Maven went to the East Village, looking for new ideas, and found out that you could get these really cool old Hush Puppies at a certain thrift store, for a very good price, and told his friends, who bought the shoes for themselves because there is something about the personal, disinterested, expert opinion of a Maven that makes us all sit up and listen. And why are the Zagat restaurant guides so popular? Partly it is because they are a convenient guide to all the restaurants in a given town. But their real power derives from the fact that the reviews are the reports of volunteers — of diners who want to share their opinions with others. Somehow that represents a more compelling recommendation than the opinion of an expert whose job it is to rate restaurants.

When I was talking to Alpert, I happened to mention that I was going to be in Los Angeles in a few weeks. "There is a place I really like, in Westwood," he said, without hesitation. "The Century Wilshire. It's a European bed-and-breakfast. They have very nice rooms. A heated pool. Underground parking. Last time I was there, five, six years ago, rooms started in the seventies and junior suites were a hundred and ten. They'll give you a rate for a week. They've got an 800 number." Since he was, after all, the Ur-Maven, I stayed at the Century Wilshire when I was in L.A., and it was everything he said it was and more. Within a few weeks of coming home, I had — completely out of character, I might add — recommended the Century Wilshire to two friends of mine, and within the month two more, and as I began to imagine how many people of those I told about the hotel had told about the hotel, and how many people like me Mark Alpert had himself told about the hotel, I realized that I had stepped into the middle of a little Mark Alpert–generated, word-of-mouth epidemic. Alpert, of course, probably doesn't know as many people as a Connector like Roger Horchow, so he doesn't quite have the same raw transmission power. But then again, if

Roger Horchow talked to you on the eve of a trip to Los Angeles, he might not give you advice on where to stay. Alpert always would. And if Horchow did make a recommendation, you might take him up on it or you might not. You would take the advice as seriously as you take advice from any friend. But if Mark Alpert gave you advice, you would *always* take it. A Connector might tell ten friends where to stay in Los Angeles, and half of them might take his advice. A Maven might tell five people where to stay in Los Angeles but make the case for the hotel so emphatically that all of them would take his advice. These are different personalities at work, acting for different reasons. But they both have the power to spark word-of-mouth epidemics.

9.

The one thing that a Maven is not is a persuader. Alpert's motivation is to educate and to help. He's not the kind of person who wants to twist your arm. As we talked, in fact, there were several key moments when he seemed to probe me for information, to find out what I knew, so he could add it to his own formidable database. To be a Maven is to be a teacher. But it is also, even more emphatically, to be a student. Mavens are really information brokers, sharing and trading what they know. For a social epidemic to start, though, some people are actually going to have to be persuaded to do something. A good number of the young people who bought Hush Puppies, for instance, were people who once upon a time wouldn't have been caught dead in them. Similarly, after Paul Revere had passed on his news, you can imagine that all of the men in the militia movement gathered around and made plans to confront the British the following morning. But it can't have been an automatic process. Some people were probably gung ho. Some may have doubted the wisdom of confronting a trained, professional army with a homegrown militia. Others — who may not have known Revere personally — might have been skeptical about the accuracy of his information. That almost everyone, in the end, fell in line is something that we would normally credit to peer pressure. But peer pressure is not always an automatic or an unconscious process. It means, as often as not, that someone actually went up to one of his peers and pressured him. In a social epidemic, Mavens are data banks. They provide the message. Connectors are social glue: they spread it. But there is also a select group of people — Salesmen — with the skills to persuade us when we are unconvinced of what we are hearing, and they are as critical to the tipping of word-of-mouth epidemics as the other two groups. Who are these Salesmen? And what makes them so good at what they do?

Tom Gau is a financial planner in Torrance, California, just south of Los Angeles. His firm — Kavesh and Gau — is the biggest in its field in southern California and one of the top financial planning firms in the country. He makes millions of dollars a year. Donald Moine, a behavioral psychologist who has written widely on the subject of persuasion, told me to look up Gau because Gau is "mesmerizing." And so he is. Tom Gau happens to sell financial planning services. But he could, if he wanted to, sell absolutely anything. If we want to understand the persuasive personality type, Gau seems a good place to start.

Gau is in his forties. He is good-looking, without being pretty at all. He is of medium height, lean, with slightly shaggy dark hair, a mustache, and a little bit of a hangdog expression. Give him a horse and a hat and he'd make an excellent cowboy. He looks like the actor Sam Elliot. When we met, Gau shook my hand. But as he told me later, usually when he meets someone he gives him a hug or — if it is a woman — a big kiss. As you would expect from a great salesman, he has a kind of natural exuberance.

"I love my clients, okay? I'll bend over backwards for them," Gau said. "I call my clients my family. I tell my clients, I've got two families. I've got my wife and my kids and I've got you." Gau talks quickly, but in fits and starts. He's always revving up and gearing down. Sometimes when he is making an aside he will rev up even further, as if to put in his own verbal parentheses. He asks lots of rhetorical questions. "I love my job. I love my job. I'm a workaholic. I get here at six and seven in the morning. I get out at nine at night. I manage a lot of money. I'm one of the top producers in the nation. But I don't tell my clients that. I'm not here because of that. I'm here to help people. I love helping people. I don't have to work anymore. I'm financially independent. So why am I here working these long hours? Because I love helping people. I love people. It's called a relationship."

Gau's pitch is that his firm offers clients a level of service and expertise they'll have difficulty getting anywhere else. Across the hall from his office is a law firm, affiliated with Kavesh and Gau, that handles wills and living trusts and all other legal matters related to financial planning. Gau has insurance specialists to handle insurance needs and stockbrokers to handle investments and retirement specialists for older clients. His arguments are rational and coherent. Moine has put together, in cooperation with Gau, what he calls a financial planner's script book. Moine's argument is that what separates a great salesman from an average one is the number and quality of answers they have to the objections commonly raised by potential clients. He sat down with Gau, then, and tape-recorded all of Gau's answers and wrote them up in a book. Moine and Gau calculate that there are about twenty questions or statements that a planner needs to be prepared for. For example: "I can do it myself" is one, and for that the script book lists fifty potential answers. "Aren't you concerned about making the wrong moves and having no one there to help you?" for instance. Or "I'm sure you do a good job at money management. However, did you know most wives outlive their husbands? If something should happen to you, would she be able to handle everything by herself?"

I can imagine someone buying this script book and memorizing each of these potential responses. I can also imagine that same person, over time, getting familiar enough with the material that he begins to judge, very well, what kinds of responses work best with what kinds of people. If you transcribed that person's interactions with his clients, he would sound just like Tom Gau because he would be using all of Tom Gau's words. According to the

standard ways by which we measure persuasiveness —
by the logic and appropriateness of the persuader's arguments — that should make the people using the script
book every bit as persuasive as Tom Gau. But is that really
true? What was interesting about Gau is the extent to
which he seemed to be persuasive in a way quite different
from the content of his words. He seems to have some
kind of indefinable trait, something powerful and contagious and irresistible that goes beyond what comes out of
his mouth, that makes people who meet him want to agree
with him. It's energy. It's enthusiasm. It's charm. It's lika-
bility. It's all those things and yet something more. At
one point I asked him whether he was happy, and he
fairly bounced off his chair.

"Very. I'm probably the most optimistic person you
could ever imagine. You take the most optimistic person
you know and take it to the hundredth power, that's me.
Because you know what, the power of positive thinking
will overcome so many things. There are so many people
who are negative. Someone will say, you can't do that.
And I'll say, what do you mean I can't do that? We moved
up to Ashland, Oregon, a little over five years ago. We
found a house we really liked. It had been on the market
for some time and it was a bit expensive. So I said to my
wife, you know what, I'm going to make a ridiculously
low offer. And she said, they're never going to take that.
I said, maybe not. What have we got to lose? The worst
thing they can say is no. I'm not going to insult them. I'm
going to give them my little pitch of here's why I'm doing
this. I'm going to make it clear what I'm suggesting. And
you know what? They accepted the offer." As Gau told

me this story, I had no difficulty at all seeing him back in Ashland, somehow convincing the seller to part with his beautiful home for a ridiculous price. "Gosh darn it," Gau said, "if you don't try, you'll never succeed."

10.

The question of what makes someone — or something — persuasive is a lot less straightforward than it seems. We know it when we see it. But just what "it" is is not always obvious. Consider the following two examples, both drawn from the psychological literature. The first is an experiment that took place during the 1984 presidential campaign between Ronald Reagan and Walter Mondale. For eight days before the election, a group of psychologists led by Brian Mullen of Syracuse University videotaped the three national nightly news programs, which then, as now, were anchored by Peter Jennings at ABC, Tom Brokaw at NBC, and Dan Rather at CBS. Mullen examined the tapes and excerpted all references to the candidates, until he had 37 separate segments, each roughly two and a half seconds long. Those segments were then shown, with the sound turned off, to a group of randomly chosen people, who were asked to rate the facial expressions of each newscaster in each segment. The subjects had no idea what kind of experiment they were involved with, or what the newscasters were talking about. They were simply asked to score the emotional content of the expressions of these three men on a 21-point scale, with the lowest being "extremely negative" and the highest point on the scale "extremely positive."

The results were fascinating. Dan Rather scored 10.46 — which translates to an almost perfectly neutral expression — when he talked about Mondale, and 10.37 when he talked about Reagan. He looked the same when he talked about the Republican as he did when he talked about the Democrat. The same was true for Brokaw, who scored 11.21 for Mondale and 11.50 for Reagan. But Peter Jennings of ABC was much different. For Mondale, he scored 13.38. But when he talked about Reagan, his face lit up so much he scored 17.44. Mullen and his colleagues went out of their way to try to come up with an innocent explanation for this. Could it be, for example, that Jennings is just more expressive in general than his colleagues? The answer seemed to be no. The subjects were also shown control segments of the three newscasters, as they talked about unequivocally happy or sad subjects (the funeral of Indira Gandhi; a breakthrough in treating a congenital disease). But Jennings didn't score any higher on the happy subjects or lower on the sad subjects than his counterparts. In fact, if anything, he seemed to be the least expressive of the three. It also isn't the case that Jennings is simply someone who has a happy expression on his face all the time. Again, the opposite seemed to be true. On the "happy" segments inserted for comparison purposes, he scored 14.13, which was substantially lower than both Rather and Brokaw. The only possible conclusion, according to the study, is that Jennings exhibited a "significant and noticeable bias in facial expression" toward Reagan.

Now here is where the study gets interesting. Mullen and his colleagues then called up people in a number of cities around the country who regularly watch the evening network news and asked them who they voted for. In every case, those who watched ABC voted for Reagan in far greater numbers than those who watched CBS or NBC. In Cleveland, for example, 75 percent of ABC watchers voted Republican, versus 61.9 percent of CBS or NBC viewers. In Williamstown, Massachusetts, ABC viewers were 71.4 percent for Reagan versus 50 percent for the other two networks; in Erie, Pennsylvania, the difference was 73.7 percent to 50 percent. The subtle pro-Reagan bias in Jennings's face seems to have influenced the voting behavior of ABC viewers.

As you can imagine, ABC News disputes this study vigorously. ("It's my understanding that I'm the only social scientist to have the dubious distinction of being called a 'jackass' by Peter Jennings," says Mullen.) It is hard to believe. Instinctively, I think, most of us would probably assume that the causation runs in the opposite direction, that Reagan supporters are drawn to ABC because of Jennings's bias, not the other way around. But Mullen argues fairly convincingly that this isn't plausible. For example, on other, more obvious levels — like, for example, story selection — ABC was shown to be the network most hostile to Reagan, so it's just as easy to imagine hard-core Republicans deserting ABC news for the rival networks. And to answer the question of whether his results were simply a fluke, four years later, in the Michael Dukakis–George Bush campaign, Mullen repeated his experiment, with the exact same results. "Jennings showed more smiles when referring to the Republican candidate than the Democrat," Mullen said, "and again in a phone survey, viewers who watch ABC were more likely to have voted for Bush."

Here is another example of the subtleties of persuasion. A large group of students were recruited for what they were told was a market research study by a company making high-tech headphones. They were each given a headset and told that the company wanted to test to see how well they worked when the listener was in motion — dancing up and down, say, or moving his or her head. All of the students listened to songs by Linda Ronstadt and the Eagles, and then heard a radio editorial arguing that tuition at their university should be raised from its present level of $587 to $750. A third were told that while they listened to the taped radio editorial they should nod their heads vigorously up and down. The next third were told to shake their heads from side to side. The final third were the control group. They were told to keep their heads still. When they were finished, all the students were given a short questionnaire, asking them questions about the quality of the songs and the effect of the shaking. Slipped in at the end was the question the experimenters really wanted an answer to: "What do you feel would be an appropriate dollar amount for undergraduate tuition per year?"

The answers to that question are just as difficult to believe as the answers to the newscasters poll. The students who kept their heads still were unmoved by the editorial. The tuition amount that they guessed was appropriate was $582 — or just about where tuition was already. Those who shook their heads from side to side as they listened to the editorial — even though they thought they were simply testing headset quality — disagreed strongly with the proposed increase. They wanted tuition to fall on average to $467 a year. Those who were told to nod their heads up and down, meanwhile, found the editorial very persuasive. They wanted tuition to rise, on average, to $646. The simple act of moving their heads up and down, ostensibly for another reason entirely — was sufficient to cause them to recommend a policy that would take money out of their own pockets. Somehow nodding, in the end, mattered as much as Peter Jennings's smiles did in the 1984 election.

There are in these two studies, I think, very important clues as to what makes someone like Tom Gau — or, for that matter, any of the Salesmen in our lives — so effective. The first is that little things can, apparently, make as much of a difference as big things. In the headphone study, the editorial had no impact on those whose heads were still. It wasn't particularly persuasive. But as soon as listeners started nodding, it became very persuasive. In the case of Jennings, Mullen says that someone's subtle signals in favor of one politician or another usually don't matter at all. But in the particular, unguarded way that people watch the news, a little bias can suddenly go a long way. "When people watch the news, they don't intentionally filter biases out, or feel they have to argue against the expression of the newscaster," Mullen explains. "It's not like someone saying: this is a very good candidate who deserves your vote. This isn't an obvious verbal message that we automatically dig in our heels against. It's much more subtle and for that reason much more insidious, and that much harder to insulate ourselves against."

The second implication of these studies is that non-verbal cues are as or more important than verbal cues. The subtle circumstances surrounding how we say things may matter more than what we say. Jennings, after all, wasn't injecting all kinds of pro-Reagan comments in his newscasts. In fact, as I mentioned, ABC was independently observed to have been the most hostile to Reagan. One of the conclusions of the authors of the headphones study — Gary Wells of the University of Alberta and Richard Petty of the University of Missouri — was that "television advertisements would be most effective if the visual display created repetitive vertical movement of the television viewers' heads (e.g., bouncing ball)." Simple physical movements and observations can have a profound effect on how we feel and think.

The third — and perhaps most important — implication of these studies is that persuasion often works in ways that we do not appreciate. It's not that smiles and nods are subliminal messages. They are straightforward and on the surface. It's just that they are incredibly subtle. If you asked the head nodders why they wanted tuition to increase so dramatically — tuition that would come out of their own pockets — none of them would say, because I was nodding my head while I listened to that editorial. They'd probably say that it was because they found the editorial particularly insightful or intelligent. They would attribute their attitudes to some more obvious, logical cause. Similarly the ABC viewers who voted for Reagan would never, in a thousand years, tell you that they voted that way because Peter Jennings smiled every time he mentioned the President. They'd say that it was because they liked Reagan's policies, or they thought he was doing a good job. It would never have occurred to them that they could be persuaded to reach a conclusion by something so arbitrary and seemingly insignificant as a smile or a nod from a newscaster. If we want to understand what makes someone like Tom Gau so persuasive, in other words, we have to look at much more than his obvious eloquence. We need to look at the subtle, the hidden, and the unspoken.

11.

What happens when two people talk? That is really the basic question here, because that's the basic context in which all persuasion takes place. We know that people talk back and forth. They listen. They interrupt. They move their hands. In the case of my meeting with Tom Gau, we were sitting in a modest-size office. I was in a chair pulled up in front of his desk. I had my legs crossed and a pad and pen on my lap. I was wearing a blue shirt and black pants and a black jacket. He was sitting behind the desk in a high-backed chair. He was wearing a pair of blue suit pants and a crisply pressed white shirt and a red tie. Some of the time he leaned forward and planted his elbows in front of him. Other times he sat back in his chair and waved his hands in the air. Between us, on the blank surface of the desk, I placed my tape recorder. That's what you would have seen, if I showed you a videotape of our meeting. But if you had taken that videotape and slowed it down, until you were looking at our interaction in slices of a fraction of a second, you would have seen something quite different. You would have seen the two of us engaging in what can only be described as an elaborate and precise dance.

The pioneer of this kind of analysis — of what is called the study of cultural microrhythms — is a man named William Condon. In one of his most famous research projects in the 1960s he attempted to decode a four-and-a-half-second segment of film, in which a woman says to a man and a child, over dinner: "You all should come around every night. We never have had a dinnertime like this in months." Condon broke the film into individual frames, each representing about ¹⁄₄₅th of a second. Then he watched — and watched. As he describes it:

> To carefully study the organization and sequence of this, the approach must be naturalistic or ethological. You just sit and look and look and look for thousands of hours until the order in the material begins to emerge. It's like sculpturing. . . . Continued study reveals further order. When I was looking at this film over and over again, I had an erroneous view of the universe that communication takes place between people. Somehow this was the model. You send the message, somebody sends the message back. The messages go here and there and everywhere. But something was funny about this.

Condon spent a year and a half on that short segment of film, until, finally, in his peripheral vision, he saw what he had always sensed was there: "the wife turning her head exactly as the husband's hands came up." From there he picked up other micromovements, other patterns that occurred over and over again, until he realized that in addition to talking and listening, the three people around the table were also engaging in what he termed "interactional synchrony." Their conversation had a rhythmic physical dimension. Each person would, within the space of one or two or three $\frac{1}{45}$th-of-a-second frames, move a shoulder or cheek or an eyebrow or a hand, sustain that movement, stop it, change direction, and start again. And what's more, those movements were perfectly in time to each person's own words — emphasizing and underlining and elaborating on the process of articulation — so that the speaker was, in effect, dancing to his or her own speech. At the same time the other people around the table were dancing along as well, moving their faces and shoulders and hands and bodies to the same rhythm. It's not that everyone was moving the same way, any more than people dancing to a song all dance the same way. It's that the timing of stops and starts of each person's micromovements — the jump and shifts of body and face — were perfectly in harmony.

Subsequent research has revealed that it isn't just gesture that is harmonized, but also conversational rhythm. When two people talk, their volume and pitch fall into balance. What linguists call speech rate — the number of speech sounds per second — equalizes. So does what is known as latency, the period of time that lapses between the moment one speaker stops talking and the moment the other speaker begins. Two people may arrive at a conversation with very different conversational patterns. But almost instantly they reach a common ground. We all do it, all the time. Babies as young as one or two days old synchronize their head, elbow, shoulder, hip, and foot movements with the speech patterns of adults. Synchrony has even been found in the interactions of humans and apes. It's part of the way we are hardwired.

When Tom Gau and I sat across from each other in his office, then, we almost immediately fell into physical and conversational harmony. We were dancing. Even before he attempted to persuade me with his words, he had forged a bond with me with his movements and his speech. So what made my encounter with him different, so much more compelling than the conversational encounters I have every day? It isn't that Gau was deliberately trying to harmonize himself with me. Some books on salesmanship recommend that persuaders try to mirror the posture or talking styles of their clients in order to establish rapport. But that's been shown not to work. It makes people more uncomfortable, not less. It's too obviously phony.

What we are talking about is a kind of super-reflex, a fundamental physiological ability of which we are barely aware. And like all specialized human traits, some people have much more mastery over this reflex than others. Part of what it means to have a powerful or persuasive personality, then, is that you can draw others into your own rhythms and dictate the terms of the interaction. In some studies, students who have a high degree of synchrony with their teachers are happier, more enthused, interested, and easygoing. What I felt with Gau was that I was being seduced, not in the sexual sense, of course, but in a global way, that our conversation was being conducted on his terms, not mine. I felt I was becoming synchronized with him. "Skilled musicians know this, and good speakers," says Joseph Cappella, who teaches at the Annenberg

School of Communication at the University of Pennsylvania. "They know when the crowds are with them, literally in synchrony with them, in movements and nods and stillness in moments of attention." It is a strange thing to admit, because I didn't want to be drawn in. I was on guard against it. But the essence of Salesmen is that, on some level, they cannot be resisted. "Tom can build a level of trust and rapport in five to ten minutes that most people will take half an hour to do," Moine says of Gau.

There is another, more specific dimension to this. When two people talk, they don't just fall into physical and aural harmony. They also engage in what is called motor mimicry. If you show people pictures of a smiling face or a frowning face, they'll smile or frown back, although perhaps only in muscular changes so fleeting that they can only be captured with electronic sensors. If I hit my thumb with a hammer, most people watching will grimace: they'll mimic my emotional state. This is what is meant, in the technical sense, by empathy. We imitate each other's emotions as a way of expressing support and caring and, even more basically, as a way of communicating with each other.

In their brilliant 1994 book *Emotional Contagion*, the psychologists Elaine Hatfield and John Cacioppo and the historian Richard Rapson go one step further. Mimicry, they argue, is also one of the means by which we infect each other with our emotions. In other words, if I smile and you see me and smile in response — even a microsmile that takes no more than several milliseconds — it's not just you imitating or empathizing with me. It may also be a way that I can pass on my happiness to you. Emotion is contagious. In a way, this is perfectly intuitive. All of us have had our spirits picked up by being around somebody in a good mood. If you think about this closely, though, it's quite a radical notion. We normally think of the expressions on our face as the reflection of an inner state. I feel happy, so I smile. I feel sad, so I frown. Emotion goes inside-out. Emotional contagion, though, suggests that the opposite is also true. If I can make you smile, I can make you happy. If I can make you frown, I can make you sad. Emotion, in this sense, goes outside-in.

If we think about emotion this way — as outside-in, not inside-out — it is possible to understand how some people can have an enormous amount of influence over others. Some of us, after all, are very good at expressing emotions and feelings, which means that we are far more emotionally contagious than the rest of us. Psychologists call these people "senders." Senders have special personalities. They are also physiologically different. Scientists who have studied faces, for example, report that there are huge differences among people in the location of facial muscles, in their form, and also — surprisingly — even in their prevalence. "It is a situation not unlike in medicine," says Cacioppo. "There are carriers, people who are very expressive, and there are people who are especially susceptible. It's not that emotional contagion is a disease. But the mechanism is the same."

Howard Friedman, a psychologist at the University of California at Riverside, has developed what he calls the Affective Communication Test to measure this ability to send emotion, to be contagious. The test is a self-administered survey, with thirteen questions relating to things like whether you can keep still when you hear good dance music, how loud your laugh is, whether you touch friends when you talk to them, how good you are at sending seductive glances, whether you like to be the center of attention. The highest possible score on the test is 117 points, with the average score, according to Friedman, somewhere around 71.

What does it mean to be a high-scorer? To answer that, Friedman conducted a fascinating experiment. He picked a few dozen people who had scored very high on his test — above 90 — and a few dozen who scored very low — below 60 — and asked them all to fill out a questionnaire measuring how they felt "at this instant." He then put all of the high-scorers in separate rooms, and paired each of them with two low-scorers. They were told to sit in the room together for two minutes. They could look at each other, but not talk. Then, once the session was over, they were asked again to fill out a detailed questionnaire on how they were feeling. Friedman found that in just two minutes, without a word being spoken, the low-scorers ended up picking up the moods of the high-scorers. If the charismatic person started out depressed, and the inexpressive person started out happy, by the end of the two minutes the inexpressive person was depressed as well. But it didn't work the other way. Only the charismatic person could infect the other people in the room with his or her emotions.

Is this what Tom Gau did to me? The thing that strikes me most about my encounter with him was his voice. He had the range of an opera singer. At times, he would sound stern. (His favorite expression in that state: "Excuse me?") At times, he would drawl, lazily and easily. At other times, he would chuckle as he spoke, making his words sing with laughter. In each of those modes his face would light up accordingly, moving, easily and deftly, from one state to another. There was no ambiguity in his presentation. Everything was written on his face. I could not see my own face, of course, but my guess is that it was a close mirror of his. It is interesting, in this context, to think back on the experiment with the nodding and the headphones. There was an example of someone persuaded from the outside-in, of an external gesture affecting an internal decision. Was I nodding when Tom Gau nodded? And shaking my head when Gau shook his head? Later, I called Gau up and asked him to take Howard Friedman's charisma test. As we went through the list, question by question, he started chuckling. By question 11 — "I am terrible at pantomime, as in games like charades" — he was laughing out loud. "I'm great at that! I always win at charades!" Out of a possible 117 points, he scored 116.

12.

In the early hours of April 19, 1775, the men of Lexington, Massachusetts, began to gather on the town common. They ranged in age from sixteen to sixty and were carrying a motley collection of muskets and swords and pistols. As the alarm spread that morning, their numbers were steadily swelled by groups of militia from the surrounding towns. Dedham sent four companies. In Lynn, men left on their own for Lexington. In towns further west that did not get the news until morning, farmers were in such haste to join the battle in Lexington that they literally left their plows in the fields. In many towns, virtually the whole male population was mustered for the fight. The men had no uniforms, so they wore ordinary clothes: coats to ward off the early morning chill and large-brimmed hats.

As the colonists rushed toward Lexington, the British Regulars (as they were known) were marching in formation toward the town as well. By dawn, the advancing soldiers could see figures all around them in the half-light, armed men running through the surrounding fields, outpacing the British in their rush to get to Lexington. As the Regulars neared the town center, they could hear drums beating in the distance. Finally the British came upon Lexington Common and the two sides met face-to-face: several hundred British soldiers confronting less than a hundred militia. In that first exchange, the British got the best of the colonists, gunning down seven militiamen in a brief flurry of gunshots on the common. But that was only the first of what would be several battles that day. When the British moved on to Concord, to systematically search for the cache of guns and ammunition they had been told was stored there, they would clash with the militia again, and this time they would be soundly defeated. This was the beginning of the American Revolution, a war that before it was over would claim many lives and consume the entire American colony. When the American colonists declared independence the following year, it would be hailed as a victory for an entire nation. But that is not the way it began. It began on a cold spring morning, with a word-of-mouth epidemic that spread from a little stable boy to all of New England, relying along the way on a small number of very special people: a few Salesmen and a man with the particular genius of both a Maven and a Connector.

THREE

The Stickiness Factor

SESAME STREET, BLUE'S CLUES, AND THE EDUCATIONAL VIRUS

I n the late 1960s, a television producer named Joan Gantz Cooney set out to start an epidemic. Her target was three-, four-, and five-year-olds. Her agent of infection was television, and the "virus" she wanted to spread was literacy. The show would last an hour and run five days a week, and the hope was that if that hour was contagious enough it could serve as an educational Tipping Point: giving children from disadvantaged homes a leg up once they began elementary school, spreading prolearning values from watchers to nonwatchers, infecting children and their parents, and lingering long enough to have an impact well after the children stopped watching the show. Cooney probably wouldn't have used these concepts or described her goals in precisely this way. But what she wanted to do, in essence, was create a learning epidemic to counter the prevailing epidemics of poverty and illiteracy. She called her idea *Sesame Street*.

By any measure, this was an audacious idea. Television is a great way to reach lots of people, very easily and cheaply. It entertains and dazzles. But it isn't a particularly educational medium. Gerald Lesser, a Harvard University psychologist who joined with Cooney in founding *Sesame Street,* says that when he was first asked to join the project, back in the late 1960s, he was skeptical. "I had always been very much into fitting how you teach to what you know about the child," he says. "You try to find the kid's strengths, so you can play to them. You try to understand the kid's weaknesses, so you can avoid them. Then you try and teach that individual kid's profile. . . . Television has no potential, no power to do that." Good teaching is interactive. It engages the child individually. It uses all the senses. It responds to the child. But a television is just a talking box. In experiments, children who are asked to read a passage and are then tested on it will invariably score higher than children asked to watch a video of the same subject matter. Educational experts describe television as "low involvement." Television is like a strain of the common cold that can spread like lightning through a population, but only causes a few sniffles and is gone in a day.

But Cooney and Lesser and a third partner — Lloyd Morrisett of the Markle Foundation in New York — set out to try anyway. They enlisted some of the top creative minds of the period. They borrowed techniques from television commercials to teach children about numbers. They used the live animation of Saturday morning cartoons to teach lessons about learning the alphabet. They brought in celebrities to sing and dance and star in comedy sketches that taught children about the virtues of cooperation or about their own emotions. *Sesame Street* aimed higher and tried harder than any other children's show had, and the extraordinary thing was that it worked. Virtually every time the show's educational value has been tested — and *Sesame Street* has been subject to more academic scrutiny than any television show in history — it has been proved to increase the reading and learning skills of its viewers. There are few educators and child psychologists who don't believe that the show managed to spread its infectious message well beyond the homes of those who watched the show regularly. The creators of *Sesame Street* accomplished something extraordinary, and the story of how they did that is a marvelous illustration of the second of the rules of the Tipping Point, the Stickiness Factor. They discovered that by making small but critical adjustments in how they presented ideas to preschoolers, they could overcome television's weakness as a teaching tool and make what they had to say memorable. *Sesame Street* succeeded because it learned how to make television sticky.

1.

The Law of the Few, which I talked about in the previous chapter, says that one critical factor in epidemics is the nature of the messenger. A pair of shoes or a warning or an infection or a new movie can become highly contagious and tip simply by being associated with a particular kind of person. But in all those examples, I took it as given that the message itself was something that could be passed on. Paul Revere started a word-of-mouth epidemic with the phrase "The British are coming." If he had instead gone on that midnight ride to tell people he was having a sale on the pewter mugs at his silversmith shop, even he, with all his enormous personal gifts, could not have galvanized the Massachusetts countryside.

Roger Horchow, likewise, faxed all his friends about the restaurant his daughter took him to, performing the first step in creating a word-of-mouth epidemic. But obviously, for that epidemic to take off, the restaurant itself had to remain a good restaurant. It had to be the kind of restaurant that made an impact on the people who ate there. In epidemics, the messenger matters: messengers are what make something spread. But the content of the message matters too. And the specific quality that a message needs to be successful is the quality of "stickiness." Is the message — or the food, or the movie, or the product — memorable? Is it so memorable, in fact, that it can create change, that it can spur someone to action?

Stickiness sounds as if it should be straightforward. When most of us want to make sure what we say is remembered, we speak with emphasis. We talk loudly, and we repeat what we have to say over and over again. Marketers feel the same way. There is a maxim in the advertising business that an advertisement has to be seen at least six times before anyone will remember it. That's a useful lesson for Coca-Cola or Nike, who have hundreds of millions of dollars to spend on marketing and can afford to saturate all forms of media with their message. But it's not all that useful for, say, a group of people trying to spark a literacy epidemic with a small budget and one hour of programming on public television. Are there smaller, subtler, easier ways to make something stick?

Consider the field of direct marketing. A company buys an ad in a magazine or sends out a direct mailing with a coupon attached that they want the reader to clip and mail back to them with a check for their product. Reaching the consumer with the message is not the hard part of direct marketing. What is difficult is getting consumers to stop, read the advertisement, remember it, and then act on it. To figure out which ads work the best, direct marketers do extensive testing. They might create a dozen different versions of the same ad and run them simultaneously in a dozen different cities and compare the response rates to each. Conventional advertisers have preconceived ideas about what makes an advertisement work: humor, splashy graphics, a celebrity endorser. Direct marketers, by contrast, have few such preconceptions, because the number of coupons that are mailed back or the number of people who call in on an 800 number in response to a television commercial gives them an objective, iron-clad measure of effectiveness. In the advertising world, direct marketers are the real students of stickiness, and some of the most intriguing conclusions about how to reach consumers have come from their work.

In the 1970s, for example, the legendary direct marketer Lester Wunderman had a showdown with the Madison Avenue firm McCann Erickson over the Columbia Record Club account. Columbia was then — as it is now — one of the largest mail order clubs in the world, and Wunderman had handled the company's advertising since it was formed in the 1950s. Columbia decided, however, to hire McCann to come up with a series of television commercials to support the direct-marketing print ads that Wunderman was creating. These were not late-night commercials with a toll-free 800 number. They were standard television spots designed simply to raise awareness. Understandably, Wunderman was upset. He had handled the Columbia account for twenty years and didn't like the idea of losing even a small part of the business to a competitor. Nor was he convinced that McCann's advertising would actually do Columbia any good. To settle the issue, he proposed a test. Columbia, he said, should run a full complement of the advertising created by his firm in the local editions of *TV Guide* and *Parade* magazine in twenty-six media markets around the United States. In thirteen of those markets, McCann should be allowed to air its "awareness" television commercials. In the other thirteen, Wunderman would air his own set of television commercials. Whoever's commercials created the greatest increase in response to the local *TV Guide* and *Parade* advertising would win the whole account. Columbia agreed, and after a month they tabulated the results. Responses in Wunderman's markets were up 80 percent, compared to 19.5 percent for McCann. Wunderman had won in a rout.

The key to Wunderman's success was something he called the "treasure hunt." In every *TV Guide* and *Parade* ad, he had his art director put a little gold box in the corner of the order coupon. Then his firm wrote a series of TV commercials that told the "secret of the Gold Box." Viewers were told that if they could find the gold box in their issues of *Parade* and *TV Guide,* they could write in the name of any record on the Columbia list and get that record free. The gold box, Wunderman theorized, was a kind of trigger. It gave viewers a reason to look for the ads in *TV Guide* and *Parade*. It created a connection between the Columbia message viewers saw on television and the message they read in a magazine. The gold box, Wunderman writes, "made the reader/viewer part of an interactive advertising system. Viewers were not just an audience but had become participants. It was like playing a game. . . . The effectiveness of the campaign was startling. In 1977, none of Columbia's ads in its extensive magazine schedule had been profitable. In 1978, with Gold Box television support, every magazine on the schedule made a profit, an unprecedented turnaround."

What's interesting about this story is that by every normal expectation McCann should have won the test. The gold box idea sounds like a really cheesy idea. Columbia was so skeptical of it that it took Wunderman several years to persuade them to let him try it. McCann, meanwhile, was one of the darlings of Madison Avenue, a firm renowned for its creativity and sophistication. Furthermore, McCann spent four times as much as Wunderman on media time. They bought prime-time slots for their space. Wunderman's ads were on in the wee hours of the morning. In the last chapter, I talked about how epidemics are, in part, a function of how many people a message reaches, and by that standard McCann was way ahead. McCann did all the big things right. But they didn't have that little final touch, that gold box, that would make their message stick.

If you look closely at epidemic ideas or messages, as often as not the elements that make them sticky turn out to be as small and as seemingly trivial as Wunderman's gold box. Consider, for example, the so-called fear experiments conducted by the social psychologist Howard Levanthal in the 1960s. Levanthal wanted to see if he could persuade a group of college seniors at Yale University to get a tetanus shot. He divided them up into several groups, and gave all of them a seven-page booklet explaining the dangers of tetanus, the importance of inoculation, and the fact that the university was offering free tetanus shots at the campus health center to all interested students. The booklets came in several versions. Some of the students were given a "high fear" version, which described tetanus in dramatic terms and included color photographs of a child having a tetanus seizure and other tetanus victims with urinary catheters, tracheotomy wounds, and nasal tubes. In the "low fear" version, the language describing the risks of tetanus was toned down, and the photographs were omitted. Levanthal wanted to see what impact the different booklets had on the students' attitudes toward tetanus and their likelihood of getting a shot.

The results were, in part, quite predictable. When they were given a questionnaire later, all the students appeared to be well educated about the dangers of tetanus. But those who were given the high-fear booklet were more convinced of the dangers of tetanus, more convinced of the importance of shots, and were more likely to say that they intended to get inoculated. All of those differences evaporated, however, when Levanthal looked at how many of the students actually went and got a shot. One month after the experiments, almost none of the subjects — a mere 3 percent — had actually gone to the health center to get inoculated. For some reason, the students had forgotten everything they had learned about tetanus, and the lessons they had been told weren't translating into action. The experiment didn't stick. Why not?

If we didn't know about the Stickiness Factor, we probably would conclude that something was wrong with the way the booklet explained tetanus to the students. We might wonder whether trying to scare them was the appropriate direction to take, whether there was a social stigma surrounding tetanus that inhibited students from admitting that they were at risk, or perhaps that medical care itself was intimidating to students. In any case, that only 3 percent of students responded suggested that there was a long way to go to reach the goal. But the Stickiness Factor suggests something quite different. It suggests that the problem probably wasn't with the overall conception of the message at all, and that maybe all the campaign needed was a little gold box. Sure enough, when Levanthal redid the experiment, one small change was sufficient to tip the vaccination rate up to 28 percent. It was simply including a map of the campus, with the university health building circled and the times that shots were available clearly listed.

There are two interesting results of this study. The first is that of the 28 percent who got inoculated, an equal number were from the high-fear and the low-fear group. Whatever extra persuasive muscle was found in the high-fear booklet was clearly irrelevant. The students knew, without seeing gory pictures, what the dangers of tetanus were, and what they ought to be doing. The second interesting thing is that, of course, as seniors they must have already known where the health center was, and doubtless had visited it several times already. It is doubtful that any of them would ever actually have used the map. In other words, what the tetanus intervention needed in order to tip was not an avalanche of new or additional information. What it needed was a subtle but significant change in presentation. The students needed to know how to fit the tetanus stuff into their lives; the addition of the map and the times when the shots were available shifted the booklet from an abstract lesson in medical risk — a lesson no different from the countless other academic lessons they had received over their academic career — to a practical and personal piece of medical advice. And once the advice became practical and personal, it became memorable.

There are enormous implications in Levanthal's fear experiments and Wunderman's work for Columbia Records for the question of how to start and tip social epidemics. We have become, in our society, overwhelmed by people clamoring for our attention. In just the past decade, the time devoted to advertisements in a typical hour of network television has grown from six minutes to nine minutes, and it continues to climb every year. The New York–based firm Media Dynamics estimates that the average American is now exposed to 254 different commercial messages in a day, up nearly 25 percent since the mid-1970s. There are now millions of web sites on the Internet, cable systems routinely carry over 50 channels of programming, and a glance inside the magazine section of any bookstore will tell you that there are thousands of magazines coming out each week and month, chock-full of advertising and information. In the advertising business,

· this surfeit of information is called the "clutter" problem, and clutter has made it harder and harder to get any one message to stick. Coca-Cola paid $33 million for the rights to sponsor the 1992 Olympics, but despite a huge advertising push, only about 12 percent of TV viewers realized that they were the official Olympic soft drink, and another 5 percent thought that Pepsi was the real sponsor. According to a study done by one advertising research firm, whenever there are at least four different 15-second commercials in a two-and-a-half-minute commercial time-out, the effectiveness of any one 15-second ad sinks to almost zero. Much of what we are told or read or watch, we simply don't remember. The information age has created a stickiness problem. But Levanthal and Wunderman's examples suggest that there may be simple ways to enhance stickiness and systematically engineer stickiness into a message. This is a fact of obvious importance to marketers, teachers, and managers. Perhaps no one has done more to illustrate the potential of this kind of stickiness engineering, however, than children's educational television, in particular the creators of *Sesame Street* and, later, the show it inspired, *Blue's Clues*.

2.

Sesame Street is best known for the creative geniuses it attracted, people like Jim Henson and Joe Raposo and Frank Oz, who intuitively grasped what it takes to get through to children. They were television's answer to Beatrix Potter or L. Frank Baum or Dr. Seuss. But it is a mistake to think of *Sesame Street* as a project conceived in a flash of insight. What made the show unusual, in fact, was the extent to which it was exactly the opposite of that — the extent to which the final product was deliberately and painstakingly engineered. *Sesame Street* was built about a single, breakthrough insight: that if you can hold the attention of children, you can educate them.

This may seem obvious, but it isn't. Many critics of television, to this day, argue that what's dangerous about TV is that it is addictive, that children and even adults watch it like zombies. According to this view, it is the formal features of television — violence, bright lights, loud and funny noises, quick editing cuts, zooming in and out, exaggerated action, and all the other things we associate with commercial TV — that hold our attention. In other words, we don't have to understand what we are looking at, or absorb what we are seeing, in order to keep watching. That's what many people mean when they say that television is passive. We watch when we are stimulated by all the whizzes and bangs of the medium. And we look away, or turn the channel, when we are bored.

What the pioneering television researchers of the 1960s and 1970s — in particular, Daniel Anderson at the University of Massachusetts — began to realize, however, is that this isn't how preschoolers watch TV at all. "The idea was that kids would sit, stare at the screen, and zone out," said Elizabeth Lorch, a psychologist at Amherst College. "But once we began to look carefully at what children were doing, we found out that short looks were actually more common. There was much more variation. Children didn't just sit and stare. They could divide their attention between a couple of different activities. And they weren't being random. There were predictable influences on what made them look back at the screen, and these were not trivial things, not just flash and dash." Lorch, for instance, once reedited an episode of *Sesame Street* so that certain key scenes of some of the sketches were out of order. If kids were only interested in flash and dash, that shouldn't have made a difference. The show, after all, still had songs and Muppets and bright colors and action and all the things that make *Sesame Street* so wonderful. But it did make a difference. The kids stopped watching. If they couldn't make sense of what they were looking at, they weren't going to look at it.

In another experiment, Lorch and Dan Anderson showed two groups of five-year-olds an episode of *Sesame Street*. The kids in the second group, however, were put in a room with lots of very attractive toys on the floor. As you would expect, the kids in the room without the toys watched the show about 87 percent of the time, while the kids with the toys watched only about 47 percent of the show. Kids are distracted by toys. But when they tested the two groups to see how much of the show the children remembered and understood, the scores were exactly the same. This result stunned the two researchers. Kids, they realized, were a great deal more sophisticated in the way they watched than had been imagined. "We were led to the conclusion," they wrote, "that the five-year-olds in the toys group were attending quite strategically, distributing their attention between toy play and viewing so that they looked at what for them were the most informative parts of the program. This strategy was so effective that the children could gain no more from increased attention."

If you take these two studies together — the toys study and the editing study — you reach quite a radical conclusion about children and television. Kids don't watch when they are stimulated and look away when they are bored. They watch when they understand and look away when they are confused. If you are in the business of educational television, this is a critical difference. It means if you want to know whether — and what — kids are learning from a TV show, all you have to do is to notice what they are watching. And if you want to know what kids aren't learning, all you have to do is notice what they aren't watching. Preschoolers are so sophisticated in their viewing behavior that you can determine the stickiness of children's programming by simple observation.

The head of research for *Sesame Street* in the early years was a psychologist from Oregon, Ed Palmer, whose specialty was the use of television as a teaching tool. When the Children's Television Workshop was founded in the late 1960s, Palmer was a natural recruit. "I was the only academic they could find doing research on children's TV," he says, with a laugh. Palmer was given the task of finding out whether the elaborate educational curriculum that had been devised for *Sesame Street* by its academic advisers was actually reaching the show's viewers. It was a critical task. There are those involved with *Sesame Street* who say, in fact, that without Ed Palmer the show would never have lasted through the first season.

Palmer's innovation was something he called the Distracter. He would play an episode of *Sesame Street* on a television monitor, and then run a slide show on a screen next to it, showing a new slide every seven and a half seconds.

"We had the most varied set of slides we could imagine," said Palmer. "We would have a body riding down the street with his arms out, a picture of a tall building, a leaf floating through ripples of water, a rainbow, a picture taken through a microscope, an Escher drawing. Anything to be novel, that was the idea." Preschoolers would then be brought into the room, two at a time, and told to watch the television show. Palmer and his assistants would sit slightly to the side, with a pencil and paper, quietly noting when the children were watching *Sesame Street* and when they lost interest and looked, instead, at the slide show. Every time the slide changed, Palmer and his assistants would make a new notation, so that by the end of the show they had an almost second-by-second account of what parts of the episode being tested managed to hold the viewers' attention and what parts did not. The Distracter was a stickiness machine.

"We'd take that big-sized chart paper, two by three feet, and tape several of those sheets together," Palmer says. "We had data points, remember, for every seven and a half seconds, which comes to close to four hundred data points for a single program, and we'd connect all those points with a red line so it would look like a stock market report from Wall Street. It might plummet or gradually decline, and we'd say whoa, what's going on here. At other times it might hug the very top of the chart and we'd say, wow, that segment's really grabbing the attention of the kids. We tabulated those Distracter scores in percentages. We'd have up to 100 percent sometimes. The average attention for most shows was around 85 to 90 percent. If the producers got that, they were happy. If they got around fifty, they'd go back to the drawing board."

Palmer tested other children's shows, like the *Tom and Jerry* cartoons, or *Captain Kangaroo*, and compared what sections of those shows worked with what sections of *Sesame Street* worked. Whatever Palmer learned, he fed back to the show's producers and writers, so they could fine-tune the material accordingly. One of the standard myths about children's television, for example, had always been that kids love to watch animals. "The producers would bring in a cat or an anteater or an otter and show it and let it cavort around," Palmer says. "They thought that would be interesting. But our Distracter showed that it was a bomb every time." A huge effort went into a *Sesame Street* character called the Man from Alphabet, whose specialty was puns. Palmer showed that kids hated him. He was canned. The Distracter showed that no single segment of the *Sesame Street* format should go beyond four minutes, and that three minutes was probably optimal. He forced the producers to simplify dialogue and abandon certain techniques they had taken from adult television. "We found to our surprise that our preschool audience didn't like it when the adult cast got into a contentious discussion," he remembers. "They didn't like it when two or three people would be talking at once. That's the producers' natural instinct, to hype a scene by creating confusion. It's supposed to tell you that this is exciting. The fact is that our kids turned away from that kind of situation. Instead of picking up on the signal that something exciting is going on, they picked up on the signal that something confusing is going on. And they'd lose interest.

"After the third or fourth season, I'd say it was rare that we ever had a segment below eighty-five percent. We

would almost never see something in the fifty to sixty percent range, and if we did, we'd fix it. You know Darwin's
terms about the survival of the fittest? We had a mechanism
to identify the fittest and decide what should survive."

The most important thing that Palmer ever found out
with the Distracter, though, came at the very beginning,
before *Sesame Street* was even on the air. "It was the summer of 1969 and we were a month and a half from air
date," Lesser remembers. "We decided, let's go for broke.
Let's produce five full shows — one hour each — before
we go to air and we'll see what we've got." To test the
shows, Palmer took them to Philadelphia and over the
third week of July showed them to groups of preschoolers in sixty different homes throughout the city. It was a
difficult period. Philadelphia was in the midst of a heat
wave, which made the children who were supposed to
watch the show restless and inattentive. In the same week,
as well, Apollo 11 landed on the moon, and some children — understandably — seemed to prefer that historic
moment to *Sesame Street.* Worst of all were the conclusions from Palmer's Distracter. "What we found," Lesser
says, "almost destroyed us."

The problem was that when the show was originally
conceived, the decision was made that all fantasy elements
of the show be separated from the real elements. This was
done at the insistence of many child psychologists, who
felt that to mix fantasy and reality would be misleading to
children. The Muppets, then, were only seen with other
Muppets, and the scenes filmed on Sesame Street itself
involved only real adults and children. What Palmer found
out in Philadelphia, though, was that as soon as they

switched to the street scenes, the kids lost all interest. "The street was supposed to be the glue," Lesser said. "We would always come back to the street. It pulled the show together. But it was just adults doing things and talking about stuff and the kids weren't interested. We were getting incredibly low attention levels. The kids were leaving the show. Levels would pop back up if the Muppets came back, but we couldn't afford to keep losing them like that." Lesser calls Palmer's results a "turning point in the history of *Sesame Street*. We knew that if we kept the street that way, the show was going to die. Everything was happening so fast. We had the testing in the summer, and we were going on the air in the fall. We had to figure out what to do."

Lesser decided to defy the opinion of his scientific advisers. "We decided to write a letter to all the other developmental psychologists and say, we know how you guys think about mixing fantasy and reality. But we're going to do it anyway. If we don't, we'll be dead in the water." So the producers went back and reshot all of the street scenes. Henson and his coworkers created puppets who could walk and talk with the adults of the show and could live alongside them on the street. "That's when Big Bird and Oscar the Grouch and Snuffleupagus were born," said Palmer. What we now think of as the essence of *Sesame Street* — the artful blend of fluffy monsters and earnest adults — grew out of a desperate desire to be sticky.

The Distracter, however, for all its strengths, is a fairly crude instrument. It tells you that a child understands what is happening on the screen and as a result is paying attention. But it doesn't tell you what the child understands or, more precisely, it doesn't tell you whether the child is paying attention to what he or she ought to be paying attention to.

Consider the following two *Sesame Street* segments, both of which are called visual-blending exercises — segments that teach children that reading consists of blending together distinct sounds. In one, "Hug," a female Muppet, approaches the word *HUG* in the center of the screen. She stands behind the *H*, sounding it out carefully, then moves to the *U*, and then the *G*. She does it again, moving from left to right, pronouncing each letter separately, before putting the sounds together to say "hug." As she does, the Muppet Herry Monster enters and repeats the word as well. The segment ends with the Herry Monster hugging the delighted little-girl Muppet.

In another segment, called "Oscar's Blending," Oscar the Grouch and the Muppet Crummy play a game called "Breakable Words," in which words are assembled and then taken apart. Oscar starts by calling for *C*, which pops up on the lower left corner of the screen. The letter *C*, Oscar tells Crummy, is pronounced "cuh." Then the letters *at* pop up in the lower right-hand corner and Crummy sounds the letters out — "*at*." The two go back and forth — Oscar saying "*cuh*" and Crummy "*at*" — each time faster and faster, until the sounds blend together to make *cat*. As this happens, the letters at the bottom of the screen move together as well to make "cat." The two Muppets repeat "cat" a few times and then the word drops from sight, accompanied by a crashing sound. Then the process begins again with the word *bat*.

Both of these segments are entertaining. They hold children's attention. On the Distracter, they score brilliantly. But do they actually teach the fundamentals of reading? That's a much harder question. To answer it, the producers of *Sesame Street* in the mid-1970s called in a group of researchers at Harvard University led by a psychologist named Barbara Flagg who were expert in something called eye movement photography. Eye movement research is based on the idea that the human eye is capable of focusing on only a very small area at one time — what is called a perceptual span. When we read, we are capable of taking in only about one key word and then four characters to the left and fifteen characters to the right at any one time. We jump from one of these chunks to another, pausing — or fixating — on them long enough to make sense of each letter. The reason we can focus clearly on only that much text is that most of the sensors in our eyes — the receptors that process what we see — are clustered in a small region in the very middle of the retina called the fovea. That's why we move our eyes when we read: we can't pick up much information about the shape, or the color, or the structure of words unless we focus our fovea directly on them. Just try, for example, to reread this paragraph by staring straight ahead at the center of the page. It's impossible.

If you can track where someone's fovea is moving and what they are fixating on, in other words, you can tell with extraordinary precision what they are actually looking at and what kind of information they are actually receiving. The people who make television commercials, not surprisingly, are obsessed with eye tracking. If you make a beer commercial with a beautiful model, it would be really important to know whether the average twenty-two-year-old male in your target audience fixates only on the model or eventually moves to your can of beer. *Sesame Street* went to Harvard in 1975 for the same reason. When kids watched "Oscar's Blending" or "Hug," were they watching and learning about the words, or were they simply watching the Muppets?

The experiment was conducted with twenty-one four- and five-year-olds, who were brought to the Harvard School of Education over the course of a week by their parents. One by one they were seated in an antique barber's chair with a padded headrest about three feet away from a 17-inch color television monitor. A Gulf & Western infrared Eye-View Monitor was set up just off to the left, carefully calibrated to track the fovea movements of each subject. What they found was that "Hug" was a resounding success. Seventy-six percent of all fixations were on the letters. Better still, 83 percent of all preschoolers fixated on the letters in a left-to-right sequence — mimicking, in other words, the actual reading process. "Oscar's Blending," on the other hand, was a disaster. Only 35 percent of total fixations fell on the letters. And exactly zero percent of the preschoolers read the letters from left to right. What was the problem? First, the letter shouldn't have been on the bottom of the screen because, as almost all eye movement research demonstrates, when it comes to television people tend to fixate on the center of the screen. That issue, though, is really secondary to the simple fact that the kids weren't watching the letters because they were watching Oscar. They were watching the model and not the beer can. "I remember 'Oscar's Blending,'" Flagg says. "Oscar was very active. He was really making a fuss in the background, and the word is not close to him at all. He's moving his mouth a lot, moving his hands. He has things in his hands. There is a great deal of distraction. The kids don't focus on the letters at all because Oscar is so interesting." Oscar was sticky. The lesson wasn't.

3.

This was the legacy of *Sesame Street:* If you paid careful attention to the structure and format of your material, you could dramatically enhance stickiness. But is it possible to make a show even stickier than *Sesame Street*? This was what three young television producers at the Nickelodeon Network in Manhattan asked themselves in the mid-1990s. It was a reasonable question. *Sesame Street,* after all, was a product of the 1960s, and in the intervening three decades major strides had been made in understanding how children's minds work. One of the Nickelodeon producers, Todd Kessler, had actually worked on *Sesame Street* and left the show dissatisfied. He didn't like the fast-paced "magazine" format of the show. "I love *Sesame Street,*" he says. "But I always believed that kids didn't have short attention spans, that they could easily sit still for a half an hour." He found traditional children's television too static. "Because the audience is not all that verbal or even preverbal, it is important to tell the story visually," he went on. "It's a visual medium, and to make it sink in, to make it powerful, you've got to make use of that. There is so much children's television that is all talk. The audience has a hard time keeping up with that." Kessler's colleague, Tracy Santomero, grew up on *Sesame Street* and had similar misgivings. "We wanted to learn from *Sesame Street* and take it one step further," Santomero said. "TV is a great medium for education. But people up until now haven't explored the potential of it. They've been using it in a rote way. I believed we could turn that around."

What they came up with is a show called *Blue's Clues.* It is half an hour, not an hour. It doesn't have an ensemble cast. It has just one live actor, Steve, a fresh-faced man in his early twenties in khakis and a rugby shirt who acts as the show's host. Instead of a varied, magazine format, each episode follows a single story line — the exploits of an animated dog by the name of Blue. It has a flat, two-dimensional feel, more like a video version of a picture book than a television show. The pace is deliberate. The script is punctuated with excruciatingly long pauses. There is none of the humor or wordplay or cleverness that characterizes *Sesame Street.* One of the animated characters on the show, a mailbox, is called Mailbox. Two other regular characters, a shovel and a pail, are called Shovel and Pail. And Blue, of course, the show's star, is Blue because he's the color blue. It is difficult, as an adult, to watch *Blue's Clues* and not wonder how this show could ever represent an improvement over *Sesame Street.* And yet it does. Within months of its debut in 1996, *Blue's Clues* was trouncing *Sesame Street* in the ratings. On the Distracter test, it scores higher than its rival in capturing children's attention. Jennings Bryant, an educational researcher at the University of Alabama, conducted a study of 120 children, comparing the performance of regular *Blue's Clues* watchers to watchers of other educational shows on a series of cognitive tests.

"After six months we began to get very big differences," Bryant said. "By almost all of our measures of flexible thinking and problem solving, we had statistically significant differences. If there were sixty items on the test, you might find that the *Blue's Clues* watchers were correctly identifying fifty of them, and the control group was identifying thirty-five." *Blue's Clues* may be one of the stickiest television shows ever made.

How is it that such an unprepossessing show is even stickier than *Sesame Street*? The answer is that *Sesame Street*, as good as it is, has a number of subtle but not insignificant limitations. Consider, for example, the problem created by the show's insistence on being clever. From the beginning *Sesame Street* was intended to appeal to both children and adults. The idea was that one of the big obstacles facing children — particularly children from lower-income families — was that their parents didn't encourage or participate in their education. *Sesame Street*'s creators wanted a show that mothers would watch along with their children. That's why the show is loaded with so many "adult" elements, the constant punning and pop culture references like Monsterpiece Theater or the Samuel Beckett parody "Waiting for Elmo." (The show's head writer, Lou Berger, says that the reason he applied for a job at *Sesame Street* was because of a Kermit sketch he saw while watching the show with his son in 1979. "It was one of those crazy fairy tales. They were looking for a princess in distress. Kermit ran out to this female Muppet princess and said" — and here Berger did a pitch-perfect Kermit —

"'Excuse me, are you a female princess in distress?' And she said, 'What does this look like? A pant suit?' I remember thinking, 'That's so great. I have to work there.'")

The problem is, preschoolers don't get these kinds of jokes, and the presence of the humor — like the elaborate pun on "distress" — can serve as a distraction. There is a good example of this in an episode of *Sesame Street* called "Roy" that ran on Christmas Eve in 1997. The episode opens with Big Bird running into a mail carrier, who has never been on Sesame Street before. The mail carrier hands Big Bird a package, and Big Bird is immediately puzzled: "If this is the first time you have ever been here," he asks, "how did you know I was Big Bird?"

MAIL CARRIER: Well, you have to admit, it's easy to figure out! [Gestures broadly at Big Bird]
BB: It is? [Looks at himself]. Oh, I see. The package is for Big Bird, and I'm a big bird. I forget sometimes. I'm just what my name says. Big Bird is a big bird.

Big Bird becomes sad. He realizes that everyone else has a name — like Oscar, or Snuffy — but he has only a description. He asks the mail carrier what her name is. She says Imogene.

BB: Gee, that's a nice name. [Looking to the camera, wistfully] I wish I had a real name like that, instead of one that just says what I am, as if I were an apple or a chair or something."

Thereupon begins a search by Big Bird for a new name. With the help of Snuffy, he canvases Sesame Street for suggestions — Zackledackle, Butch, Bill, Omar, Larry, Sammy, Ebenezer, Jim, Napoleon, Lancelot, Rocky — before settling on Roy. But then, once everyone starts calling him by his new name, Big Bird realizes that he doesn't like it after all. "Somehow it doesn't seem right," he says. "I think I made a big mistake." He switches back. "Even if Big Bird isn't a regular name," he concludes, "it's my name, and I like the way all my friends say it."

This was, at least on the surface, an excellent episode. The premise is challenging and conceptual, but fascinating. It deals candidly with emotion, and, unlike other children's shows, tells children that it's okay not to be happy all of the time. Most of all, it's funny.

It sounds like it should be a winner, right?

Wrong. The Roy show was tested by the *Sesame Street* research staff and the numbers were very disappointing. The first segment involving Snuffy and Big Bird did well. As you would expect, the viewers were curious. Then things began to fall apart. By the second of the street scenes, attention dropped to 80 percent. By the third, 78 percent. By the fourth 40 percent, then 50, then 20. After viewing the show, the kids were quizzed on what they had seen. "We asked very specific questions and were looking for clear answers," Rosemary Truglio, *Sesame Street*'s research head said. "What was the show about? Sixty percent knew. What did Big Bird want to do? Fifty-three percent knew. What was Big Bird's new name? Twenty percent knew. How did Big Bird feel at the end? Fifty percent knew." By comparison, another of the shows tested by *Sesame Street* at the very same time recorded 90 percent plus correct answers on the postshow quiz. The show simply wasn't making any impression. It wasn't sticking.

Why did the show fail? The problem, at root, is with the premise of the show — the essential joke that Big Bird doesn't want to be known as a big bird. That's the kind of wordplay that a preschooler simply doesn't understand. Preschoolers make a number of assumptions about words and their meaning as they acquire language, one of the most important of which is what the psychologist Ellen Markman calls the principle of mutual exclusivity. Simply put, this means that small children have difficulty believing that any one object can have two different names. The natural assumption of children, Markman argues, is that if an object or person is given a second label, then that label must refer to some secondary property or attribute of that object. You can see how useful this assumption is to a child faced with the extraordinary task of assigning a word to everything in the world. A child who learns the word *elephant* knows, with absolute certainty, that it is something different from a dog. Each new word makes the child's knowledge of the world more precise. Without mutual exclusivity, by contrast, if a child thought that elephant could simply be another label for dog, then each new word would make the world seem more complicated. Mutual exclusivity also helps the child think clearly. "Suppose," Markman writes, "a child who already knows 'apple' and 'red' hears someone refer to an apple as 'round.' By mutual exclusivity, the child can eliminate the object (apple) and its color (red) as the meaning of 'round' and can try to analyze the object for some other property to label."

What this means, though, is that children are going to have trouble with objects that have two names, or objects that change names. A child has difficulty with, say, the idea that an oak is both an oak and a tree; he or she may well assume that in that case "tree" is a word for collection of oaks.

The idea, then, that Big Bird no longer wants to be called Big Bird but instead wants to be called Roy is almost guaranteed to befuddle a preschooler. How can someone with one name decide to have another name? Big Bird is saying that Big Bird is merely a descriptive name of the type of animal he is, and that he wants a particular name. He doesn't want to be a tree. He wants to be an oak. But three- and four-year-olds don't understand that a tree can also be an oak. To the extent that they understand what is going on at all, they probably think that Big Bird is trying to change into something else — into some other kind of animal, or some other collection of animals. And how could he do that?

There's a deeper problem. *Sesame Street* is a magazine show. A typical show consists of at least forty distinct segments, none more than about three minutes — street scenes with the actors and Muppets, animation, and short films from outside the studio. With shows like "Roy," in the late 1990s, the writers of the show attempted, for the first time, to link some of these pieces together with a common theme. For most of the show's history, though, the segments were entirely autonomous; in fact new *Sesame* shows were constructed, for the most part, by mixing together fresh street scenes with animated bits and filmed sequences from the show's archives.

The show's creators had a reason for wanting to construct *Sesame Street* this way. They thought preschoolers did not have the attention span to handle anything other than very short, tightly focused segments. "We looked at the viewing patterns of young children, and we found that they were watching *Laugh-In*," says Lloyd Morrisett, who was one of the show's founders. "That had a very strong effect on the early *Sesame Street*. Zany, relatively quick one-liners. The kids seemed to love it." *Sesame Street*'s creators were impressed even more by the power of television commercials. The sixties were the golden age of Madison Avenue, and at the time it seemed to make perfect sense that if a 60-second television spot could sell breakfast cereal to a four-year-old, then it could also sell that child the alphabet. Part of the appeal of Jim Henson and the Muppets to the show's creators, in fact, was that in the 1960s Henson had been running a highly successful advertising shop. Many of the most famous Muppets were created for ad campaigns: Big Bird is really a variation of a seven-foot dragon created by Henson for La Choy commercials; Cookie Monster was a pitchman for Frito-Lay; Grover was used in promotional films for IBM. (Henson's Muppet commercials from the 50s and 60s are hysterically funny but have a dark and edgy quality that understandably was absent from his *Sesame Street* work.)

"I think the most significant format feature in a commercial is that it's about one thing," said Sam Gibbon, one of the earliest *Sesame Street* producers. "It's about selling one idea. The notion of breaking down the production of *Sesame Street* into units small enough so they could address a single educational goal like an individual letter owed a lot to that technique of commercials."

But is the commercial theory of learning true? Daniel Anderson says that new research suggests that children actually don't like commercials as much as we thought they did because commercials "don't tell stories, and stories have a particular salience and importance to young people." The original *Sesame Street* was anti-narrative: it was, by design, an unconnected collection of sketches. "It wasn't just the ads that influenced the early *Sesame Street*," Anderson says. "There was also a theoretical perspective at the time, based in part on [the influential child psychologist] Piaget, that a preschool child couldn't follow an extended narrative." Since the late 1960s, however, this idea has been turned on its head. At three and four and five, children may not be able to follow complicated plots and subplots. But the narrative form, psychologists now believe, is absolutely central to them. "It's the only way they have of organizing the world, of organizing experience," Jerome Bruner, a psychologist at New York University, says. "They are not able to bring theories that organize things in terms of cause and effect and relationships, so they turn things into stories, and when they try to make sense of their life they use the storied version of their experience as the basis for further reflection. If they don't catch something in a narrative structure, it doesn't get remembered very well, and it doesn't seem to be accessible for further kinds of mulling over."

Bruner was involved, in the early 1980s, in a fascinating project — called "Narratives from the Crib" — that was critical in changing the views of many child experts.

The project centered on a two-year-old girl from New Haven called Emily, whose parents — both university professors — began to notice that before their daughter went to sleep at night she talked to herself. Curious, they put a small microcassette recorder in her crib and, several nights a week, for the next fifteen months, recorded both the conversations they had with Emily as they put her to bed and the conversations she had with herself before she fell asleep. The transcripts — 122 in all — were then analyzed by a group of linguists and psychologists led by Katherine Nelson of Harvard University. What they found was that Emily's conversations with herself were more advanced than her conversations with her parents. In fact, they were significantly more advanced. One member of the team that met to discuss the Emily tapes, Carol Fleisher Feldman, later wrote:

> In general, her speech to herself is so much richer and more complex [than her speech to adults] that it has made all of us, as students of language development, begin to wonder whether the picture of language acquisition offered in the literature to date does not underrepresent the actual patterns of the linguistic knowledge of the young child. For once the lights are out and her parents leave the room, Emily reveals a stunning mastery of language forms we would never have suspected from her [everyday] speech.

Feldman was referring to things like vocabulary and grammar and — most important — the structure of Emily's monologues. She was making up stories, narratives, that explained and organized the things that happened to her. Sometimes these stories were what linguists call temporal narratives. She would create a story to try to integrate events, actions, and feelings into one structure — a process that is a critical part of a child's mental development. Here is a story Emily told herself at 32 months, which I will quote at length to emphasize just how sophisticated children's speech is when they are by themselves:

> Tomorrow when we wake up from bed, first me and Daddy and Mommy, you, eat breakfast eat breakfast like we usually do, and then we're going to play and then soon as Daddy comes, Carl's going to come over, and then we're going to play a little while. And then Carl and Emily are both going down the car with somebody, and we're going to ride to nursery school [whispered], and then when we get there, we're all going to get out of the car, go into nursery school, and Daddy's going to give us kisses, then go, and then say, and then we will say goodbye, then he's going to work and we're going to play at nursery school. Won't that be funny? Because sometimes I go to nursery school cause it's a nursery school day. Sometimes I stay with Tanta all week. And sometimes we play mom and dad. But usually, sometimes, I, um, oh go to nursery school. But today I'm going to nursery school in the morning. In the morning, Daddy in the, when and usual, we're going to eat breakfast like we usually do, and then we're going to . . . and then we're going to . . . play. And then we're, then the doorbell's going to ring, and here comes Carl in here, and then Carl, and then we are all going to play, and then . . .

Emily is describing her Friday routine. But it's not a particular Friday. It's what she considers an ideal Friday, a hypothetical Friday in which everything she wants to happen happens. It is, as Bruner and Joan Lucariello write in their commentary on the segment,

> a remarkable act of world making . . . she uses tonal emphasis, prolongation of key words, and a kind of "re-enactment" reminiscent of the we-are-there cinema verité (with her friend Carl practically narrated through the door as he enters). As if to emphasize that she has everything "down pat" she delivers the monologue in a rhythmic, almost singsong way. And in the course of the soliloquy, she even feels free to comment on the drollness of the course that events are taking ("Won't that be funny").

It is hard to look at this evidence of the importance of narrative and not marvel at the success of *Sesame Street.* Here was a show that eschewed what turns out to be the most important of all ways of reaching young children. It also diluted its appeal to preschoolers with jokes aimed only at adults. Yet it succeeded anyway. That was the genius of *Sesame Street,* that through the brilliance of its writing and the warmth and charisma of the Muppets it managed to overcome what might otherwise have been overwhelming obstacles. But it becomes easy to understand how you would make a children's show even stickier than *Sesame Street.* You'd make it perfectly literal, without any word-play or comedy that would confuse preschoolers. And you'd teach kids how to think in the same way that kids teach themselves how to think — in the form of the story. You would make, in other words, *Blue's Clues.*

4.

Every episode of *Blue's Clues* is constructed the same way. Steve, the host, presents the audience with a puzzle involving Blue, the animated dog. In one show the challenge is to figure out Blue's favorite story. In another, it is to figure out Blue's favorite food. To help the audience unlock the puzzle, Blue leaves behind a series of clues, which are objects tattooed with one of his paw prints. In between the discovery of the clues, Steve plays a series of games — mini-puzzles — with the audience that are thematically related to the overall puzzle. In the show about Blue's favorite story, for example, one of the mini-puzzles involves Steve and Blue sitting down with the Three Bears, whose bowls of porridge have been mixed up, and enlisting the audience's help in matching the small, middle, and large bowls with Mama, Papa, and Baby Bear. As the show unfolds, Steve and Blue move from one animated set to another, from a living room to a garden to fantastical places, jumping through magical doorways, leading viewers on a journey of discovery, until, at the end of the story, Steve returns to the living room. There, at the climax of every show, he sits down in a comfortable chair to think — a chair known, of course, in the literal world of *Blue's Clues*, as the Thinking Chair. He puzzles over Blue's three clues and attempts to come up with the answer.

This much is, obviously, a radical departure from *Sesame Street*. But having turned their back on that part of the *Sesame Street* legacy, the creators of *Blue's Clues* then went back and borrowed those parts of *Sesame Street* that they thought did work. In fact, they did more than borrow. They took those sticky elements and tried to make them even stickier. The first was the idea that the more kids are engaged in watching something — intellectually and physically — the more memorable and meaningful it becomes. "I'd noticed that some segments on *Sesame Street* elicited a lot of interaction from kids, where the segments asked for it," says Daniel Anderson, who worked with Nickelodeon in designing *Blue's Clues.* "Something that stuck in my mind was when Kermit would hold his finger to the screen and draw an animated letter, you'd see kids holding their fingers up and drawing a letter along with him. Or occasionally, when a *Sesame Street* character would ask a question, you'd hear kids answer out loud. But *Sesame Street* just somehow never took that idea and ran with it. They knew that kids did this some of the time, but they never tried to build a show around that idea. Nickelodeon did some pilot shows before *Blue's Clues* where kids would be explicitly asked to participate, and lo and behold, there was a lot of evidence that they would. So putting these ideas together, that kids are interested in being intellectually active when they watch TV, and given the opportunity they'll be behaviorally active, that created the philosophy for *Blue's Clues.*"

Steve, as a result, spends almost all his time on screen talking directly at the camera. When he enlists the audience's help, he actually enlists the audience's help. Often, there are close-ups of his face, so it is as if he is almost in the room with his audience. Whenever he asks a question, he pauses. But it's not a normal pause. It's a preschooler's pause, several beats longer than any adult would ever wait for an answer. Eventually an unseen studio audience yells out a response. But the child at home is given the opportunity to shout out an answer of his own. Sometimes Steve will play dumb. He won't be able to find a certain clue that might be obvious to the audience at home and he'll look beseechingly at the camera. The idea is the same: to get the children watching to verbally participate, to become actively involved. If you watch *Blue's Clues* with a group of children, the success of this strategy is obvious. It's as if they're a group of diehard Yankees fans at a baseball game.

The second thing that *Blue's Clues* took from *Sesame Street* was the idea of repetition. This was something that had fascinated the CTW pioneers. In the five pilot shows that Palmer and Lesser took to Philadelphia in 1969, there was a one-minute bit called Wanda the Witch that used the *w* sound over and over: Wanda the Witch wore a wig in the windy winter in Washington, etc., etc. "We didn't know how much we could repeat elements," Lesser says. "We put it in three times on the Monday, three times on the Tuesday, three times on the Wednesday, left it out on Thursday, then put it in right at the end of the Friday show. Some of the kids toward the end of the day Wednesday were saying, not Wanda the Witch again. When Wanda the Witch came back Friday, they jumped and clapped. Kids reach a saturation point. But then nostalgia sets in."

Not long afterward (and quite by accident), the *Sesame Street* writers figured out why kids like repetition so much. The segment in question this time featured the actor James Earl Jones reciting the alphabet. As originally taped, Jones took long pauses between letters, because the idea was to insert other elements between the letters. But Jones, as you can imagine, cut such a compelling figure that the *Sesame Street* producers left the film as it was and played it over and over again for years: the letter *A* or *B*, etc., would appear on the screen, there would be a long pause, and then Jones would boom out the name and the letter would disappear. "What we noticed was that the first time through, kids would shout out the name of the letter after Jones did," Sam Gibbon says. "After a couple of repetitions, they would respond to the appearance of the letter before he did, in the long pause. Then, with enough repetitions, they would anticipate the letter before it appeared. They were sequencing themselves through the piece; first they learned the name of the letter, then they learned to associate the name of the letter with its appearance, then they learned the sequence of letters." An adult considers constant repetition boring, because it requires reliving the same experience over and again. But to preschoolers repetition isn't boring, because each time they watch something they are experiencing it in a completely different way. At CTW, the idea of learning through repetition was called the James Earl Jones effect.

Blue's Clues is essentially a show built around the James Earl Jones effect. Instead of running new episodes one after another, and then repeating them as reruns later in the seasons – like every other television show — Nickelodeon runs the same *Blue's Clues* episode for five straight days, Monday through Friday, before going on to the next one. As you can imagine, this wasn't an idea that came easily to Nickelodeon. Santomero and Anderson had to convince them. (It also helped that Nickelodeon didn't have the money to produce a full season of *Blue's Clues* shows.) "I had the pilot in my house, and at the time my daughter was three and a half and she kept watching it over and over again," Anderson says. "I kept track. She watched it fourteen times without any lagging of enthusiasm." When the pilot was taken out into the field for testing, the same thing happened. They showed it five days in a row to a large group of preschoolers, and attention and comprehension actually increased over the course of the week — with the exception of the oldest children, the five-year-olds, whose attention fell off at the very end. Like the kids watching James Earl Jones, the children responded to the show in a different way with each repeat viewing, becoming more animated and answering more of Steve's questions earlier and earlier. "If you think about the world of a preschooler, they are surrounded by stuff they don't understand — things that are novel. So the driving force for a preschooler is not a search for novelty, like it is with older kids, it's a search for understanding and predictability," says Anderson. "For younger kids, repetition is really valuable. They demand it. When they see a show over and over again, they not only are understanding it better, which is a form of power, but just by predicting what is going to happen, I think they feel a real sense of affirmation and self-worth. And *Blue's Clues* doubles that feeling, because they also feel like they are participating in something. They feel like they are helping Steve."

Of course, kids don't always like repetition. Whatever they are watching has to be complex enough to allow, upon repeated exposure, for deeper and deeper levels of comprehension. At the same time, it can't be so complex that the first time around it baffles the children and turns them off. In order to strike this balance, *Blue's Clues* engages in much of the same kind of research as *Sesame Street* — but at a far more intense level. Where *Sesame Street* tests a given show only once — and after it's completed — *Blue's Clues* tests shows three times before they go on the air. And while *Sesame Street* will typically only test a third of its episodes, *Blue's Clues* tests them all.

I accompanied the *Blue's Clues* research team on one of their weekly excursions to talk to preschoolers. They were led by Alice Wilder, director of research for the show, a lively dark-haired woman who had just finished her doctorate in education at Columbia University. With her were two others, both women in their early twenties — Alison Gilman and Allison Sherman. On the morning that I joined them they were testing a proposed script at a preschool in Greenwich Village.

The script being tested was about animal behavior. It was, essentially, a first draft, laid out in a picture book that roughly corresponded to the way the actual episode would unfold, scene by scene, on television. The *Blue's Clues* tester played the part of Steve, and walked the kids through the script, making a careful note of all the questions they answered correctly and those that seemed to baffle them. At one point, for example, Sherman sat down with a towheaded five-year-old named Walker and a four-and-a-half-year-old named Anna in a purple-and-white checked skirt. She began reading from the script. Blue had a favorite animal. Would they help us find out what it was? The kids were watching her closely. She began going through some of the subsidiary puzzles, one by one. She showed them a picture of an anteater.

"What does an anteater eat?" she asked.

Walker said, "Ants."

Sherman turned the page to a picture of an elephant. She pointed at its trunk.

"What's that?"

Walker peered in. "A trunk."

She pointed at the tusks. "Do you know what the white things are?"

Walker looked again. "Nostrils."

She showed them a picture of a bear, then came the first Blue's clue, a little splotch of white and black tattooed with one of Blue's paw prints.

"That's black and white," Anna said.

Sherman looked at the two of them. "What animal could Blue want to learn about?" She paused. Anna and Walker looked puzzled. Finally Walker broke the silence: "We had better go to the next clue."

The second round of puzzles was a little harder. There was a picture of a bird. The kids were asked what the bird was doing — the answer was singing — and then why it was doing that. They talked about beavers and worms and then came to the second Blue's clue — an iceberg. Anna and Walker were still stumped. On they went to the third round, a long discussion of fish. Sherman showed them a picture of a little fish lying camouflaged at the bottom of the sea, eying a big fish.

"Why is the fish hiding?" Sherman asked.

WALKER: "Because of the giant fish."

ANNA: "Because he will eat him."

They came to the third Blue's clue. It was a cardboard cutout of one of Blue's paw prints. Sherman took the paw print and moved it toward Walker and Anna, wiggling it as she did.

"What's this doing?" she asked.

Walker screwed up his face in concentration. "It's walking like a human," he said.

"Is it wriggling like a human?" Sherman asked.

"It's waddling," Anna said.

Sherman went over the clues in order: black and white, ice, waddling.

There was a pause. Suddenly Walker's face lit up. "It's a penguin!" He was shouting with the joy of discovery. "A penguin's black and white. It lives on the ice and it waddles!"

Blue's Clues succeeds as a story of discovery only if the clues are in proper order. The show has to start out easy — to give the viewers confidence — and then get progressively harder and harder, challenging the preschoolers more and more, drawing them into the narrative. The first set of puzzles about anteaters and elephants had to be easier than the set of puzzles about beavers and worms, which in turn had to be easier than the final set about fish. The layering of the show is what makes it possible for a child to watch the show four and five times: on each successive watching they master more and more, guessing correctly deeper into the program, until, by the end, they can anticipate every answer.

After the morning of testing, the *Blue's Clues* team sat down and went through the results of the puzzles, one by one. Thirteen out of the 26 children guessed correctly that anteaters ate ants, which wasn't a good response rate for the first clue. "We like to open strong," Wilder said. They continued on, rustling through their papers. The results of a puzzle about beavers drew a frown from Wilder. When shown a picture of a beaver dam, the kids did badly on answering the first question — what is the beaver doing? — but very well (19 out of 26) on the second question, why is he doing it? "The layers are switched," Wilder said. She wanted the easier question first. On to the fish questions: Why was the little fish hiding from the big fish? Sherman looked up from her notes. "I had a great answer. 'The little fish didn't want to scare the big fish.' That's why he was hiding." They all laughed.

Finally, came the most important question. Was the order of Blue's clues correct? Wilder and Gilman had presented the clues in the order that the script had stipulated: ice, waddle, then black and white. Four of the 17 kids they talked to guessed penguin after the first clue, six more guessed it after the second clue and four after all three clues. Wilder then turned to Sherman, who had given her clues in a different order: black and white, ice, waddle.

"I had no correct answers out of nine kids after one clue," she reported. "After ice, I was one of nine, and after waddle I was six of nine."

"Your clincher clue was waddle? That seems to work," Wilder responded. "But along the way were they guessing lots of different things?"

"Oh yes," Sherman said. "After one clue, I had guesses of dogs, cows, panda bears, and tigers. After ice, I got polar bears and cougars."

Wilder nodded. Sherman's clue order got the kids thinking as broadly as possible early in the show, but still preserved the suspense of penguin until the end. The clue order they had — the clue order that seemed the best back when they were writing the script — gave the answer away far too soon. Sherman's clue order had suspense. The original order did not. They had spent a morning with a group of kids and come away with just what they wanted. It was only a small change. But a small change is often all that it takes.

There is something profoundly counterintuitive in the definition of stickiness that emerges from all these examples. Wunderman stayed away from prime-time slots for his commercials and bought fringe time, which goes against every principle of advertising. He eschewed slick "creative" messages for a seemingly cheesy "Gold Box" treasure hunt. Levanthal found that the hard sell — that trying to scare students into getting tetanus shots — didn't work, and what really worked was giving them a map they didn't need directing them to a clinic that they already knew existed. *Blue's Clues* got rid of the cleverness and originality that made *Sesame Street* the most beloved television program of its generation, created a plodding, literal show, and repeated each episode five times in a row.

We all want to believe that the key to making an impact on someone lies with the inherent quality of the ideas we present. But in none of these cases did anyone substantially alter the content of what they were saying. Instead, they tipped the message by tinkering, on the margin, with the presentation of their ideas, by putting the Muppet behind the *H-U-G*, by mixing Big Bird with the adults, by repeating episodes and skits more than once, by having Steve pause just a second longer than normal after he asks a question, by putting a tiny gold box in the corner of the ad. The line between hostility and acceptance, in other words, between an epidemic that tips and one that does not, is sometimes a lot narrower than it seems. The creators of *Sesame Street* did not junk their entire show after the Philadelphia disaster. They just added Big Bird, and he made all the difference in the world. Howard Levanthal didn't redouble his efforts to terrify his students into getting a tetanus shot. He just threw in a map and a set of appointment times. The Law of the Few says that there are exceptional people out there who are capable of starting epidemics. All you have to do is find them. The lesson of stickiness is the same. There is a simple way to package information that, under the right circumstances, can make it irresistible. All you have to do is find it.

FOUR

The Power of Context (Part One)

O n December 22, 1984, the Saturday before Christmas, Bernhard Goetz left his apartment in Manhattan's Greenwich Village and walked to the IRT subway station at Fourteenth Street and Seventh Avenue. He was a slender man in his late thirties, with sandy-colored hair and glasses, dressed that day in jeans and a windbreaker. At the station, he boarded the number two downtown express train and sat down next to four young black men. There were about twenty people in the car, but most sat at the other end, avoiding the four teenagers, because they were, as eyewitnesses would say later, "horsing around" and "acting rowdy." Goetz seemed oblivious. "How are ya?" one of the four, Troy Canty, said to Goetz, as he walked in. Canty was lying almost prone on one of the subway benches. Canty and another of the teenagers, Barry Allen, walked up to Goetz and asked him for five dollars. A third youth, James

Ramseur, gestured toward a suspicious-looking bulge in his pocket, as if he had a gun in there.

"What do you want?" Goetz asked.

"Give me five dollars," Canty repeated.

Goetz looked up and, as he would say later, saw that Canty's "eyes were shiny, and he was enjoying himself. . . . He had a big smile on his face," and somehow that smile and those eyes set him off. Goetz reached into his pocket and pulled out a chrome-plated five-shot Smith and Wesson .38, firing at each of the four youths in turn. As the fourth member of the group, Darrell Cabey, lay screaming on the ground, Goetz walked over to him and said, "You seem all right. Here's another," before firing a fifth bullet into Cabey's spinal cord and paralyzing him for life.

In the tumult, someone pulled the emergency brake. The other passengers ran into the next car, except for two women who remained riveted in panic. "Are you all right?" Goetz asked the first, politely. Yes, she said. The second woman was lying on the floor. She wanted Goetz to think she was dead. "Are you all right?" Goetz asked her, twice. She nodded yes. The conductor, now on the scene, asked Goetz if he was a police officer.

"No," said Goetz. "I don't know why I did it." Pause. "They tried to rip me off."

The conductor asked Goetz for his gun. Goetz declined. He walked through the doorway at the front of the car, unhooked the safety chain, and jumped down onto the tracks, disappearing into the dark of the tunnel.

In the days that followed, the shooting on the IRT caused a national sensation. The four youths all turned out to have criminal records. Cabey had been arrested previously for armed robbery, Canty for theft. Three of them had screwdrivers in their pockets. They seemed the embodiment of the kind of young thug feared by nearly all urban-dwellers, and the mysterious gunman who shot them down seemed like an avenging angel. The tabloids dubbed Goetz the "Subway Vigilante" and the "Death Wish Shooter." On radio call-in shows and in the streets, he was treated as a hero, a man who had fulfilled the secret fantasy of every New Yorker who had ever been mugged or intimidated or assaulted on the subway. On New Year's Eve, a week after the shooting, Goetz turned himself in to a police station in New Hampshire. Upon his extradition to New York City, the *New York Post* ran two pictures on its front page: one of Goetz, handcuffed and head bowed, being led into custody, and one of Troy Canty — black, defiant, eyes hooded, arms folded — being released from the hospital. The headline read, "Led Away in Cuffs While Wounded Mugger Walks to Freedom." When the case came to trial, Goetz was easily acquitted on charges of assault and attempted murder. Outside Goetz's apartment building, on the evening of the verdict, there was a raucous, impromptu street party.

1.

The Goetz case has become a symbol of a particular, dark moment in New York City history, the moment when the city's crime problem reached epidemic proportions. During the 1980s, New York City averaged well over 2,000 murders and 600,000 serious felonies a year. Underground, on the subways, conditions could only be described as chaotic. Before Bernie Goetz boarded the number two train that day, he would have waited on a dimly lit platform, surrounded on all sides by dark, damp, graffiti-covered walls. Chances are his train was late, because in 1984 there was a fire somewhere on the New York system every day and a derailment every other week. Pictures of the crime scene, taken by police, show that the car Goetz sat in was filthy, its floor littered with trash and the walls and ceiling thick with graffiti, but that wasn't unusual because in 1984 every one of the 6,000 cars in the Transit Authority fleet, with the exception of the midtown shuttle, was covered with graffiti — top to bottom, inside and out. In the winter, the cars were cold because few were adequately heated. In the summer, the cars were stiflingly hot because none were air-conditioned. Today, the number two train accelerates to over 40 miles an hour as it rumbles toward the Chambers Street express stop. But it's doubtful Goetz's train went that fast. In 1984, there were 500 "red tape" areas on the system — places where track damage had made it unsafe for trains to go more than 15 miles per hour. Fare-beating was so commonplace that it was costing the Transit Authority as much as $150 million in lost revenue annually. There were about 15,000 felonies on the system a year — a number that would hit 20,000 a year by the end of the decade — and harassment of riders by panhandlers and petty criminals was so pervasive that ridership of the trains had sunk to its lowest level in the history of the subway system. William Bratton, who was later to be a key figure in New York's successful fight against violent crime, writes in his autobiography of riding the New York subways in the

1980s after living in Boston for years, and being stunned at what he saw:

> After waiting in a seemingly endless line to buy a token, I tried to put a coin into a turnstile and found it had been purposely jammed. Unable to pay the fare to get into the system, we had to enter through a slam gate being held open by a scruffy-looking character with his hand out; having disabled the turnstiles, he was now demanding that riders give him their tokens. Meanwhile, one of his cohorts had his mouth on the coin slots, sucking out the jammed coins and leaving his slobber. Most people were too intimidated to take these guys on: Here, take the damned token, what do I care? Other citizens were going over, under, around, or through the stiles for free. It was like going into the transit version of Dante's *Inferno*.

This was New York City in the 1980s, a city in the grip of one of the worst crime epidemics in its history. But then, suddenly and without warning, the epidemic tipped. From a high in 1990, the crime rate went into precipitous decline. Murders dropped by two-thirds. Felonies were cut in half. Other cities saw their crime drop in the same period. But in no place did the level of violence fall farther or faster. On the subways, by the end of the decade, there were 75 percent fewer felonies than there had been at the decade's start. In 1996, when Goetz went to trial a second time, as the defendant in a civil suit brought by Darrell Cabey, the case was all but ignored by the press, and Goetz himself seemed almost an anachronism. At a time when New York had become the safest big city in the country, it seemed hard to remember precisely what it was that Goetz had once symbolized. It was simply inconceivable that someone could pull a gun on someone else on the subway and be called a hero for it.

2.

This idea of crime as an epidemic, it must be said, is a little strange. We talk about "epidemics of violence" or crime waves, but it's not clear that we really believe that crime follows the same rules of epidemics as, say, Hush Puppies did, or Paul Revere's ride. Those epidemics involved relatively straightforward and simple things — a product and a message. Crime, on the other hand, isn't a single discrete thing, but a word used to describe an almost impossibly varied and complicated set of behaviors. Criminal acts have serious consequences. They require the criminal to do something that puts himself at great personal peril. To say someone is a criminal is to say that he or she is evil or violent or dangerous or dishonest or unstable or any combination of any of those things — none of which is a psychological state that would seem to be transmitted, casually, from one person to another. Criminals do not, in other words, sound like the kind of people who could be swept up by the infectious winds of an epidemic. Yet somehow, in New York City, this is exactly what occurred. In the years between the beginning and the middle of the 1990s, New York City did not get a population transplant. Nobody went out into the streets and successfully taught every would-be delinquent the distinction between right and wrong. There were just as many psychologically damaged people, criminally inclined people, living in the city at the peak of the crime wave as in the trough. But for some reason tens of thousands of those people suddenly stopped committing crimes. In 1984, an encounter between an angry subway rider and four young black youths led to bloodshed. Today, in New York's subways, that same encounter doesn't lead to violence anymore. How did that happen?

The answer lies in the third of the principles of epidemic transmission, the Power of Context. The Law of the Few looked at the kinds of people who are critical in spreading information. The chapter on *Sesame Street* and *Blue's Clues* looked at the question of Stickiness, suggesting that in order to be capable of sparking epidemics, ideas have to be memorable and move us to action. We've looked at the people who spread ideas, and we've looked at the characteristics of successful ideas. But the subject of this chapter — the Power of Context — is no less important than the first two. Epidemics are sensitive to the conditions and circumstances of the times and places in which they occur. In Baltimore, syphilis spreads far more in the summer than in the winter. Hush Puppies took off because they were being worn by kids in the cutting-edge precincts of the East Village — an environment that helped others to look at the shoes in a new light. It could even be argued that the success of Paul Revere's ride — in some way — owed itself to the fact that it was made at night. At night, people are home in bed, which makes them an awful lot easier to reach than if they are off on errands or working in the fields. And if someone wakes us up to tell us something, we automatically assume the news is going to be urgent. One can only imagine how "Paul Revere's afternoon ride" might have compared.

This much, I think, is relatively straightforward. But the lesson of the Power of Context is that we are more than just sensitive to changes in context. We're exquisitely sensitive to them. And the kinds of contextual changes that are capable of tipping an epidemic are very different than we might ordinarily suspect.

3.

During the 1990s violent crime declined across the United States for a number of fairly straightforward reasons. The illegal trade in crack cocaine, which had spawned a great deal of violence among gangs and drug dealers, began to decline. The economy's dramatic recovery meant that many people who might have been lured into crime got legitimate jobs instead, and the general aging of the population meant that there were fewer people in the age range — males between eighteen and twenty-four — that is responsible for the majority of all violence. The question of why crime declined in New York City, however, is a little more complicated. In the period when the New York epidemic tipped down, the city's economy hadn't improved. It was still stagnant. In fact, the city's poorest neighborhoods had just been hit hard by the welfare cuts of the early 1990s. The waning of the crack cocaine epidemic in New York was clearly a factor, but then again, it had been in steady decline well before crime dipped. As for the aging of the population, because of heavy immigration to New York in the 1980s, the city was getting younger in the 1990s, not older. In any case, all of these trends are long-term changes that one would expect to have gradual effects. In New York the decline was anything but gradual. Something else clearly played a role in reversing New York's crime epidemic.

The most intriguing candidate for that "something else" is called the Broken Windows theory. Broken Windows was the brainchild of the criminologists James Q. Wilson and George Kelling. Wilson and Kelling argued that crime is the inevitable result of disorder. If a window is broken and left unrepaired, people walking by will conclude that no one cares and no one is in charge. Soon, more windows will be broken, and the sense of anarchy will spread from the building to the street on which it faces, sending a signal that anything goes. In a city, relatively minor problems like graffiti, public disorder, and aggressive panhandling, they write, are all the equivalent of broken windows, invitations to more serious crimes:

> Muggers and robbers, whether opportunistic or professional, believe they reduce their chances of being caught or even identified if they operate on streets where potential victims are already intimidated by prevailing conditions. If the neighborhood cannot keep a bothersome panhandler from annoying passersby, the thief may reason, It is even less likely to call the police to identify a potential mugger or to interfere if the mugging actually takes place.

This is an epidemic theory of crime. It says that crime is contagious — just as a fashion trend is contagious — that it can start with a broken window and spread to an entire community. The Tipping Point in this epidemic, though, isn't a particular kind of person — a Connector like Lois Weisberg or a Maven like Mark Alpert. It's something physical like graffiti. The impetus to engage in a certain kind of behavior is not coming from a certain kind of person but from a feature of the environment.

In the mid-1980s Kelling was hired by the New York Transit Authority as a consultant, and he urged them to put the Broken Windows theory into practice. They obliged, bringing in a new subway director by the name of David Gunn to oversee a multibillion-dollar rebuilding of the subway system. Many subway advocates, at the time, told Gunn not to worry about graffiti, to focus on the larger questions of crime and subway reliability, and it seemed like reasonable advice. Worrying about graffiti at a time when the entire system was close to collapse seems as pointless as scrubbing the decks of the *Titanic* as it headed toward the icebergs. But Gunn insisted. "The graffiti was symbolic of the collapse of the system," he says. "When you looked at the process of rebuilding the organization and morale, you had to win the battle against graffiti. Without winning that battle, all the management reforms and physical changes just weren't going to happen. We were about to put out new trains that were worth about ten million bucks apiece, and unless we did something to protect them, we knew just what would happen. They would last one day and then they would be vandalized."

Gunn drew up a new management structure and a precise set of goals and timetables aimed at cleaning the system line by line, train by train. He started with the number seven train that connects Queens to midtown Manhattan, and began experimenting with new techniques to clean off the paint. On stainless-steel cars, solvents were used. On the painted cars, the graffiti were simply painted over. Gunn made it a rule that there should be no retreat, that once a car was "reclaimed" it should never be allowed to be vandalized again. "We were religious about it," Gunn said. At the end of the number one line in the Bronx, where the trains stop before turning around and going back to Manhattan, Gunn set up a cleaning station. If a car came in with graffiti, the graffiti had to be removed during the changeover, or the car was removed from service. "Dirty" cars, which hadn't yet been cleansed of graffiti, were never to be mixed with "clean" cars. The idea was to send an unambiguous message to the vandals themselves.

"We had a yard up in Harlem on one hundred thirty-fifth Street where the trains would lay up over night," Gunn said. "The kids would come the first night and paint the side of the train white. Then they would come the next night, after it was dry, and draw the outline. Then they would come the third night and color it in. It was a three-day job. We knew the kids would be working on one of the dirty trains, and what we would do is wait for them to finish their mural. Then we'd walk over with rollers and paint it over. The kids would be in tears, but we'd just be going up and down, up and down. It was a message to them. If you want to spend three nights of your time vandalizing a train, fine. But it's never going to see the light of day."

Gunn's graffiti cleanup took from 1984 to 1990. At that point, the Transit Authority hired William Bratton to head the transit police, and the second stage of the reclamation of the subway system began. Bratton was, like Gunn, a disciple of Broken Windows. He describes

Kelling, in fact, as his intellectual mentor, and so his first step as police chief was as seemingly quixotic as Gunn's. With felonies — serious crimes — on the subway system at an all-time high, Bratton decided to crack down on fare-beating. Why? Because he believed that, like graffiti, fare-beating could be a signal, a small expression of disorder that invited much more serious crimes. An estimated 170,000 people a day were entering the system, by one route or another, without paying a token. Some were kids, who simply jumped over the turnstiles. Others would lean backward on the turnstiles and force their way through. And once one or two or three people began cheating the system, other people — who might never otherwise have considered evading the law — would join in, reasoning that if some people weren't going to pay, they shouldn't either, and the problem would snowball. The problem was exacerbated by the fact fare-beating was not easy to fight. Because there was only $1.25 at stake, the transit police didn't feel it was worth their time to pursue it, particularly when there were plenty of more serious crimes happening down on the platform and in the trains.

Bratton is a colorful, charismatic man, a born leader, and he quickly made his presence felt. His wife stayed behind in Boston, so he was free to work long hours, and he would roam the city on the subway at night, getting a sense of what the problems were and how best to fight them. First, he picked stations where fare-beating was the biggest problem, and put as many as ten policemen in plainclothes at the turnstiles. The team would nab fare-beaters one by one, handcuff them, and leave them standing, in a daisy chain, on the platform until they had a "full catch." The idea was to signal, as publicly as possible, that the transit police were now serious about cracking down on fare-beaters. Previously, police officers had been wary of pursuing fare-beaters because the arrest, the trip to the station house, the filling out of necessary forms, and the waiting for those forms to be processed took an entire day — all for a crime that usually merited no more than a slap on the wrist. Bratton retrofitted a city bus and turned it into a rolling station house, with its own fax machines, phones, holding pen, and fingerprinting facilities. Soon the turnaround time on an arrest was down to an hour. Bratton also insisted that a check be run on all those arrested. Sure enough, one out of seven arrestees had an outstanding warrant for a previous crime, and one out of twenty was carrying a weapon of some sort. Suddenly it wasn't hard to convince police officers that tackling fare-beating made sense. "For the cops it was a bonanza," Bratton writes. "Every arrest was like opening a box of Cracker Jack. What kind of toy am I going to get? Got a gun? Got a knife? Got a warrant? Do we have a murderer here? . . . After a while the bad guys wised up and began to leave their weapons home and pay their fares." Under Bratton, the number of ejections from subway stations — for drunkenness, or improper behavior — tripled within his first few months in office. Arrests for misdemeanors, for the kind of minor offenses that had gone unnoticed in the past, went up fivefold between 1990 and 1994. Bratton turned the transit police into an organization focused on the smallest infractions, on the details of life underground.

After the election of Rudolph Giuliani as mayor of New York in 1994, Bratton was appointed head of the

New York City Police Department, and he applied the same strategies to the city at large. He instructed his officers to crack down on quality-of-life crimes: on the "squeegee men" who came up to drivers at New York City intersections and demanded money for washing car windows, for example, and on all the other above-ground equivalents of turnstile-jumping and graffiti. "Previous police administration had been handcuffed by restrictions," Bratton says. "We took the handcuffs off. We stepped up enforcement of the laws against public drunkenness and public urination and arrested repeat violators, including those who threw empty bottles on the street or were involved in even relatively minor damage to property. . . . If you peed in the street, you were going to jail." When crime began to fall in the city — as quickly and dramatically as it had in the subways — Bratton and Giuliani pointed to the same cause. Minor, seemingly insignificant quality-of-life crimes, they said, were Tipping Points for violent crime.

Broken Windows theory and the Power of Context are one and the same. They are both based on the premise that an epidemic can be reversed, can be tipped, by tinkering with the smallest details of the immediate environment. This is, if you think about it, quite a radical idea. Think back, for instance, to the encounter between Bernie Goetz and those four youths on the subway: Allen, Ramseur, Cabey, and Canty. At least two of them, according to some reports, appear to have been on drugs at the time of the incident. They all came from the Claremont Village housing project in one of the worst parts of the South Bronx. Cabey was, at the time, under indictment for armed robbery. Canty had a prior felony arrest for possession of stolen property. Allen had been previously arrested for attempted assault. Allen, Canty, and Ramseur also all had misdemeanor convictions, ranging from criminal mischief to petty larceny. Two years after the Goetz shooting, Ramseur was sentenced to twenty-five years in prison for rape, robbery, sodomy, sexual abuse, assault, criminal use of a firearm, and possession of stolen property. It's hard to be surprised when people like this wind up in the middle of a violent incident.

Then there's Goetz. He did something that is completely anomalous. White professionals do not, as a rule, shoot young black men on the subway. But if you look closely at who he was, he fits the stereotype of the kind of person who ends up in violent situations. His father was a strict disciplinarian with a harsh temper, and Goetz was often the focus of his father's rage. At school, he was the one teased by classmates, the last one picked for school games, a lonely child who would often leave school in tears. He worked, after graduating from college, for Westinghouse, building nuclear submarines. But he didn't last long. He was constantly clashing with his superiors over what he saw as shoddy practices and corner-cutting, and sometimes broke company and union rules by doing work that he was contractually forbidden to do. He took an apartment on Fourteenth Street in Manhattan, near Sixth Avenue, on a stretch of city block that was then heavy with homelessness and drug dealing. One of the doormen in the building, with whom Goetz was close, was beaten badly by muggers. Goetz became obsessed with cleaning up the neighborhood. He complained endlessly about a

vacant newsstand near his building, which was used by
vagrants as a trash bin and stank of urine. One night, mysteriously, it burned down, and the next day Goetz was out
on the street sweeping away the debris. Once at a community meeting, he said, to the shock of others in the room,
"The only way we're going to clean up this street is to get
rid of the spics and niggers." In 1981, Goetz was mugged
by three black youths as he entered the Canal Street station one afternoon. He ran out of the station with the
three of them in pursuit. They grabbed the electronics
equipment he was carrying, beat him, and threw him up
against a plate-glass door, leaving him with permanent
damage to his chest. With the help of an off-duty sanita-
tion worker, Goetz managed to subdue one of his three
attackers. But the experience left him embittered. He had
to spend six hours in the station house, talking to police,
while his assailant was released after two hours and
charged, in the end, with only a misdemeanor. He applied
to the city for a gun permit. He was turned down. In Sep-
tember 1984, his father died. Three months later, he sat
down next to four black youths on the subway and started
shooting.

Here, in short, was a man with an authority problem,
with a strong sense that the system wasn't working, who
had been the recent target of humiliation. Lillian Rubin,
Goetz's biographer, writes that his choice to live on Fourteenth Street could hardly have been an accident. "For
Bernie," she writes, "there seems to be something seductive about the setting. Precisely because of its deficits and
discomforts, it provided him with a comprehensible target
for the rage that lives inside him. By focusing it on the

external world, he need not deal with his internal one. He rails about the dirt, the noise, the drunks, the crime, the pushers, the junkies. And all with good reason." Goetz's bullets, Rubin concludes, were "aimed at targets that existed as much in his past as in the present."

If you think of what happened on the number two train this way, the shooting begins to feel inevitable. Four hoodlums confront a man with apparent psychological problems. That the shooting took place on the subway seems incidental. Goetz would have shot those four kids if he had been sitting in a Burger King. Most of the formal explanations we use for criminal behavior follow along the same logic. Psychiatrists talk about criminals as people with stunted psychological development, people who have had pathological relationships with their parents, who lack adequate role models. There is a relatively new literature that talks about genes that may or may not dispose certain individuals to crime. On the popular side, there are endless numbers of books by conservatives talking about crime as a consequence of moral failure — of communities and schools and parents who no longer raise children with a respect for right and wrong. All of those theories are essentially ways of saying that the criminal is a personality type — a personality type distinguished by an insensitivity to the norms of normal society. People with stunted psychological development don't understand how to conduct healthy relationships. People with genetic predispositions to violence fly off the handle when normal people keep their cool. People who aren't taught right from wrong are oblivious to what is and what is not appropriate behavior. People who grow up poor, fatherless, and buffeted by racism don't have the same commitment to social norms as those from healthy middle-class homes. Bernie Goetz and those four thugs on the subway were, in this sense, prisoners of their own, dysfunctional, world.

But what do Broken Windows and the Power of Context suggest? Exactly the opposite. They say that the criminal — far from being someone who acts for fundamental, intrinsic reasons and who lives in his own world — is actually someone acutely sensitive to his environment, who is alert to all kinds of cues, and who is prompted to commit crimes based on his perception of the world around him. That is an incredibly radical — and in some sense unbelievable — idea. There is an even more radical dimension here. The Power of Context is an environmental argument. It says that behavior is a function of social context. But it is a very strange kind of environmentalism. In the 1960s, liberals made a similar kind of argument, but when they talked about the importance of environment they were talking about the importance of fundamental social factors: crime, they said, was the result of social injustice, of structural economic inequities, of unemployment, of racism, of decades of institutional and social neglect, so that if you wanted to stop crime you had to undertake some fairly heroic steps. But the Power of Context says that what really matters is little things. The Power of Context says that the showdown on the subway between Bernie Goetz and those four youths had very little to do, in the end, with the tangled psychological pathology of Goetz, and very little as well to do with the background and poverty of the four youths who accosted him, and everything to do with the message sent by the graffiti on the walls and the disorder at the turnstiles. The Power of Context says you don't have to solve the big problems to solve crime. You can prevent crimes just by scrubbing off graffiti and arresting fare-beaters: crime epidemics have Tipping Points every bit as simple and straightforward as syphilis in Baltimore or a fashion trend like Hush Puppies. This is what I meant when I called the Power of Context a radical theory. Giuliani and Bratton — far from being conservatives, as they are commonly identified — actually represent on the question of crime the most extreme liberal position imaginable, a position so extreme that it is almost impossible to accept. How can it be that what was going on in Bernie Goetz's head doesn't matter? And if it is really true that it doesn't matter, why is that fact so hard to believe?

4.

In chapter 2, when I was discussing what made someone like Mark Alpert so important in word-of-mouth epidemics, I talked about two seemingly counterintuitive aspects of persuasion. One was the study that showed how people who watched Peter Jennings on ABC were more likely to vote Republican than people who watched either Tom Brokaw or Dan Rather because, in some unconscious way, Jennings was able to signal his affection for Republican candidates. The second study showed how people who were charismatic could — without saying anything and with the briefest of exposures — infect others with their emotions. The implications of those two studies go to the heart of the Law of the Few, because they suggest that what we think of as inner states — preferences and emotions — are actually powerfully and imperceptibly influenced by seemingly inconsequential personal influences, by a newscaster we watch for a few minutes a day or by someone we sit next to, in silence, in a two-minute experiment. The essence of the Power of Context is that the same thing is true for certain kinds of environments — that in ways that we don't necessarily appreciate, our inner states are the result of our outer circumstances. The field of psychology is rich with experiments that demonstrate this fact. Let me give you just a few examples.

In the early 1970s, a group of social scientists at Stanford University, led by Philip Zimbardo, decided to create a mock prison in the basement of the university's psychology building. They took a thirty-five-foot section of corridor and created a cell block with a prefabricated wall. Three small, six- by nine-foot cells were created from laboratory rooms and given steel-barred, black-painted doors. A closet was turned into a solitary confinement cell. The group then advertised in the local papers for volunteers, men who would agree to participate in the experiment. Seventy-five people applied, and from those Zimbardo and his colleagues picked the 21 who appeared the most normal and healthy on psychological tests. Half of the group were chosen, at random, to be guards, and were given uniforms and dark glasses and told that their responsibility was to keep order in the prison. The other half were told that they were to be prisoners. Zimbardo got the Palo Alto Police Department to "arrest" the prisoners in their homes, cuff them, bring them to the station house, charge them with a fictitious crime, fingerprint them, then blindfold them and bring them to the prison in the Psychology Department basement. Then they were stripped and given a prison uniform to wear, with a number on the front and back that was to serve as their only means of identification for the duration of their incarceration.

The purpose of the experiment was to try to find out why prisons are such nasty places. Was it because prisons are full of nasty people, or was it because prisons are such nasty environments that they make people nasty? In the answer to that question is obviously the answer to the question posed by Bernie Goetz and the subway cleanup, which is how much influence does immediate environment have on the way people behave? What Zimbardo found out shocked him. The guards, some of whom had previously identified themselves as pacifists, fell quickly into the role of hard-bitten disciplinarians. The first night they woke up the prisoners at two in the morning and made them do pushups, line up against the wall, and perform other arbitrary tasks. On the morning of the second day, the prisoners rebelled. They ripped off their numbers and barricaded themselves in their cells. The guards responded by stripping them, spraying them with fire extinguishers, and throwing the leader of the rebellion into solitary confinement. "There were times when we were pretty abusive, getting right in their faces and yelling at them," one guard remembers. "It was part of the whole atmosphere of terror." As the experiment progressed, the guards got systematically crueler and more sadistic. "What we were unprepared for was the intensity of the change and the speed at which it happened," Zimbardo says. The guards were making the prisoners say to one another they loved each other, and making them march down the hallway, in handcuffs, with paper bags over their heads. "It was completely the opposite from the way I conduct myself now," another guard remembers. "I think I was positively creative in terms of my mental cruelty." After 36 hours, one prisoner began to get hysterical, and had to be released. Four more then had to be released because of "extreme emotional depression, crying, rage, and acute anxiety." Zimbardo had originally intended to have the experiment run for two weeks. He called it off after six days. "I realize now," one prisoner said after the experiment was over, "that no matter how together I thought I was inside my head, my prisoner behavior was often less under my control than I realized." Another said: "I began to feel that I was losing my identity, that the person I call ————, the person who volunteered to get me into this prison (because it was a prison to me, it still is a prison to me, I don't regard it as an experiment or a simulation . . .) was distant from me, was remote, until finally I wasn't that person. I was 416. I was really my number and 416 was really going to have to decide what to do."

Zimbardo's conclusion was that there are specific situations so powerful that they can overwhelm our inherent predispositions. The key word here is situation. Zimbardo isn't talking about environment, about the major external influences on all of our lives. He's not denying that how we are raised by our parents affects who we are, or that the kind of schools we went to, the friends we have, or the neighborhoods we live in affect our behavior. All of these things are undoubtedly important. Nor is he denying that our genes play a role in determining who we are. Most psychologists believe that nature — genetics — accounts for about half of the reason why we tend to act the way we do. His point is simply that there are certain times and places and conditions when much of that can be swept away, that there are instances where you can take normal people from good schools and happy families and good neighborhoods and powerfully affect their behavior merely by changing the immediate details of their situation.

This same argument was made, perhaps more explicitly, in the 1920s in a landmark set of experiments by two New York–based researchers, Hugh Hartshorne and M. A. May. Hartshorne and May took as their subjects about eleven thousand schoolchildren between the ages of eight and sixteen, and over the course of several months they gave them literally dozens of tests, all designed to measure honesty. The types of tests that Hartshorne and May used are quite central to their conclusion, so I'll identify a number of them in some detail.

One set, for example, was simple aptitude tests developed by the Institute for Educational Research, a precursor to the group that now develops the SATs. In the sentence-completion test, children were asked to fill in words that had been left blank For example: "The poor little——has——nothing to——; he is hungry." In the arithmetic test, children were given math questions like "When sugar costs 10 cents a pound, how much will five pounds cost" and asked to write their answers in the margin. The tests were given in only a fraction of the time usually needed for completion, so most children had lots of unanswered questions, and when the time was up the tests were collected and graded. The following day the students were given the same kinds of tests again, with questions that were different but of equal difficulty. This time, though, the students were given an answer key and, under minimal supervision, told to grade their own papers. Hartshorne and May, in other words, had set up a sting operation. With the answers in hand and lots of unanswered questions, the students had ample opportunity to cheat. And with the previous day's tests in hand, Hartshorne and May could compare the first day's answers to the second, and get a good sense of how much each student was cheating.

Another set of tests was what are called speed tests, much simpler measures of ability. Students were given 56 pairs of numbers and told to add them. Or they were shown a sequence of several hundred randomly arranged letters of the alphabet and asked to read through them and underline all the *A*'s. Students were allowed a minute to complete each of these tests. Then they were given another set of equivalent tests, only this time the time limit wasn't enforced at all, allowing the students to keep on working if they wanted to. In all, the two psychologists administered countless different tests in countless different situations. They had children undertake tests of physical ability, like chin-ups or broad jumps, and secretly observed them to see whether they cheated in reporting how well they did. They gave students tests to do at home, where they had ample opportunity to use dictionaries or ask for help, and compared those results to how they did on similar tests administered at school, where cheating was impossible. In the end, their results fill three thick volumes and, along the way, challenge a lot of preconceptions of what character is.

Their first conclusion is, unsurprisingly, that lots of cheating goes on. In one case, the scores on tests where cheating was possible were 50 percent higher, on average, than the "honest" scores. When Hartshorne and May began to look for patterns in the cheating, some of their findings were equally obvious. Smart children cheat a little less than less-intelligent children. Girls cheat about as much as boys. Older children cheat more than younger children, and those from stable and happy homes cheat a bit less than those from unstable and unhappy homes. If you analyze the data you can find general patterns of behavioral consistency from test to test.

But the consistency isn't nearly as high as you might expect. There isn't one tight little circle of cheaters and one tight little circle of honest students. Some kids cheat at home but not at school; some kids cheat at school but not at home. Whether or not a child cheated on, say, the word completion test was not an iron-clad predictor of whether he or she would cheat on, say, the underlining A's part of the speed test. If you gave the same group of kids the same test, under the same circumstances six months apart, Hartshorne and May found, the same kids would cheat in the same ways in both cases. But once you changed any of those variables — the material on the test, or the situation in which it was administered — the kinds of cheating would change as well.

What Hartshorne and May concluded, then, is that something like honesty isn't a fundamental trait, or what they called a "unified" trait. A trait like honesty, they concluded, is considerably influenced by the situation. "Most children," they wrote,

> will deceive in certain situations and not in others. Lying, cheating, and stealing as measured by the test situations used in these studies are only very loosely related. Even cheating in the classroom is rather highly specific, for a child may cheat on an arithmetic test and not on a spelling test, etc. Whether a child will practice deceit in any given situation depends in part on his intelligence, age, home background, and the like and in part on the nature of the situation itself and his particular relation to it.

This, I realize, seems wildly counterintuitive. If I asked you to describe the personality of your best friends, you could do so easily, and you wouldn't say things like "My friend Howard is incredibly generous, but only when I ask him for things, not when his family asks him for things," or "My friend Alice is wonderfully honest when it comes to her personal life, but at work she can be very slippery." You would say, instead, that your friend Howard is generous and your friend Alice is honest. All of us, when it comes to personality, naturally think in terms of absolutes: that a person is a certain way or is not a certain way. But what Zimbardo and Hartshorne and May are suggesting is that this is a mistake, that when we think only in terms of inherent traits and forget the role of situations, we're deceiving ourselves about the real causes of human behavior.

Why do we make this mistake? It's probably the result of the way evolution has structured our brain. For instance, anthropologists who study vervets find that these kinds of monkeys are really bad at picking up the significance of things like an antelope carcass hanging in a tree (which is a sure sign that a leopard is in the vicinity) or the presence of python tracks. Vervets have been known to waltz into a thicket, ignoring a fresh trail of python tracks, and then act stunned when they actually come across the snake itself. This doesn't mean that vervets are stupid: they are very sophisticated when it comes to questions that have to do with other vervets. They can hear the call of a male vervet and recognize whether it comes from their own group or a neighboring group. If vervets hear a baby vervet's cry of distress, they will look immediately not in the direction of the baby, but at its mother — they know instantly whose baby it is. A vervet, in other words, is very good at processing certain kinds of vervetish information, but not so good at processing other kinds of information.

The same is true of humans.

Consider the following brain teaser. Suppose I give you four cards labeled with the letters *A* and *D* and the numerals 3 and 6. The rule of the game is that a card with a vowel on it always has an even number on the other side. Which of the cards would you have to turn over to prove this rule to be true? The answer is two: the A card and the three card. The overwhelming majority of people given this test, though, don't get it right. They tend to answer just the *A* card, or the *A* and the six. It's a hard question. But now let me pose another question. Suppose four people are drinking in a bar. One is drinking Coke. One is sixteen. One is drinking beer and one is twenty-five. Given the rule that no one under twenty-one is allowed to drink beer, which of those people's IDs do we have to check to make sure the law is being observed? Now the answer is easy. In fact, I'm sure that almost everyone will get it right: the beer drinker and the sixteen-year-old. But, as the psychologist Leda Cosmides (who dreamt up this example) points out, it is exactly the same puzzle as the *A, D,* 3, and 6 puzzle. The difference is that it is framed in a way that makes it about people, instead of about numbers, and as human beings we are a lot more sophisticated about each other than we are about the abstract world.

The mistake we make in thinking of character as something unified and all-encompassing is very similar to a kind of blind spot in the way we process information. Psychologists call this tendency the Fundamental Attribution Error (FAE), which is a fancy way of saying that when it comes to interpreting other people's behavior, human beings invariably make the mistake of overestimating the importance of fundamental character traits and underestimating the importance of the situation and context. We will always reach for a "dispositional" explanation for events, as opposed to a contextual explanation. In one experiment, for instance, a group of people are told to watch two sets of similarly talented basketball players, the first of whom are shooting baskets in a well-lighted gym and the second of whom are shooting baskets in a badly lighted gym (and obviously missing a lot of shots). Then they are asked to judge how good the players were. The players in the well-lighted gym were considered superior. In another example, a group of people are brought in for an experiment and told they are going to play a quiz game. They are paired off and they draw lots. One person gets a card that says he or she is going to be the "Contestant."

The other is told he or she is going to be the "Questioner." The Questioner is then asked to draw up a list of ten "challenging but not impossible" questions based on areas of particular interest or expertise, so someone who is into Ukrainian folk music might come up with a series of questions based on Ukrainian folk music. The questions are posed to the Contestant, and after the quiz is over, both parties are asked to estimate the level of general knowledge of the other. Invariably, the Contestants rate the Questioners as being a lot smarter than they themselves are.

You can do these kinds of experiments a thousand different ways and the answer almost always comes out the same way. This happens even when you give people a clear and immediate environmental explanation of the behavior they are being asked to evaluate: that the gym, in the first case, has few lights on; that the Contestant is being asked to answer the most impossibly biased and rigged set of questions. In the end, this doesn't make much difference. There is something in all of us that makes us instinctively want to explain the world around us in terms of people's essential attributes: he's a better basketball player, that person is smarter than I am.

We do this because, like vervets, we are a lot more attuned to personal cues than contextual cues. The FAE also makes the world a much simpler and more understandable place. In recent years, for example, there has been much interest in the idea that one of the most fundamental factors in explaining personality is birth order: older siblings are domineering and conservative, younger siblings more creative and rebellious. When psychologists actually try to verify this claim, however, their answers sound like the Hartshorne and May conclusions. We do reflect the influences of birth order but, as the psychologist Judith Harris points out in *The Nurture Assumption,* only around our families. When they are away from their families — in different contexts — older siblings are no more likely to be domineering and younger siblings no more likely to be rebellious than anyone else. The birth order myth is an example of the FAE in action. But you can see why we are so drawn to it. It is much easier to define people just in terms of their family personality. It's a kind of shorthand. If we constantly had to qualify every assessment of those around us, how would we make sense of the world? How much harder would it be to make the thousands of decisions we are required to make about whether we like someone or love someone or trust someone or want to give someone advice? The psychologist Walter Mischel argues that the human mind has a kind of "reducing valve" that "creates and maintains the perception of continuity even in the face of perpetual observed changes in actual behavior." He writes:

> When we observe a woman who seems hostile and fiercely independent some of the time but passive, dependent and feminine on other occasions, our reducing valve usually makes us choose between the two syndromes. We decide that one pattern is in the service of the other, or that both are in the service of a third motive. She must be a really castrating lady with a façade of passivity — or perhaps she is a warm, passive-dependent woman with a surface defense of aggressiveness. But perhaps nature is bigger than our concepts and it is possible for the lady to be a hostile, fiercely independent, passive,

dependent, feminine, aggressive, warm, castrating person all-in-one. Of course which of these she is at any particular moment would not be random or capricious — it would depend on who she is with, when, how, and much, much more. But each of these aspects of her self may be a quite genuine and real aspect of her total being.

Character, then, isn't what we think it is or, rather, what we want it to be. It isn't a stable, easily identifiable set of closely related traits, and it only seems that way because of a glitch in the way our brains are organized. Character is more like a bundle of habits and tendencies and interests, loosely bound together and dependent, at certain times, on circumstance and context. The reason that most of us seem to have a consistent character is that most of us are really good at controlling our environment. I have a lot of fun at dinner parties. As I result, I throw a lot of dinner parties and my friends see me there and think that I'm fun. But if I couldn't have lots of dinner parties, if my friends instead tended to see me in lots of different situations over which I had little or no control — like, say, faced with four hostile youths in a filthy, broken-down subway — they probably wouldn't think of me as fun anymore.

5.

Some years ago two Princeton University psychologists, John Darley and Daniel Batson, decided to conduct a study inspired by the biblical story of the Good Samaritan. As you may recall, that story, from the New Testament Gospel of Luke, tells of a traveler who has been beaten and robbed and left for dead by the side of the road from Jerusalem to Jericho. Both a priest and a Levite — worthy, pious men — came upon the man but did not stop, "passing by on the other side." The only man to help was a Samaritan — the member of a despised minority — who "went up to him and bound up his wounds" and took him to an inn. Darley and Batson decided to replicate that study at the Princeton Theological Seminary. This was an experiment very much in the tradition of the FAE, and it is an important demonstration of how the Power of Context has implications for the way we think about social epidemics of all kinds, not just violent crime.

Darley and Batson met with a group of seminarians, individually, and asked each one to prepare a short, extemporaneous talk on a given biblical theme, then walk over to a nearby building to present it. Along the way to the presentation, each student ran into a man slumped in an alley, head down, eyes closed, coughing and groaning. The question was, who would stop and help? Darley and Batson introduced three variables into the experiment, to make its results more meaningful. First, before the experiment even started, they gave the students a questionnaire about why they had chosen to study theology. Did they see religion as a means for personal and spiritual fulfillment? Or were they looking for a practical tool for finding meaning in everyday life? Then they varied the subject of the theme the students were asked to talk about. Some were asked to speak on the relevance of the professional clergy to the religious vocation. Others were given the parable of the Good Samaritan. Finally, the instructions given by the experimenters to each student varied as well.

In some of the cases, as he sent the students on their way, the experimenter would look at his watch and say, "Oh, you're late. They were expecting you a few minutes ago. We'd better get moving." In other cases, he would say, "It will be a few minutes before they're ready for you, but you might as well head over now."

If you ask people to predict which seminarians played the Good Samaritan (and subsequent studies have done just this) their answers are highly consistent. They almost all say that the students who entered the ministry to help people and those reminded of the importance of compassion by having just read the parable of the Good Samaritan will be the most likely to stop. Most of us, I think, would agree with those conclusions. In fact, neither of those factors made any difference. "It is hard to think of a context in which norms concerning helping those in distress are more salient than for a person thinking about the Good Samaritan, and yet it did not significantly increase helping behavior," Darley and Batson concluded. "Indeed, on several occasions, a seminary student going to give his talk on the parable of the Good Samaritan literally stepped over the victim as he hurried on his way." The only thing that really mattered was whether the student was in a rush. Of the group that was, 10 percent stopped to help. Of the group who knew they had a few minutes to spare, 63 percent stopped.

What this study is suggesting, in other words, is that the convictions of your heart and the actual contents of your thoughts are less important, in the end, in guiding your actions than the immediate context of your behavior. The words "Oh, you're late" had the effect of making someone who was ordinarily compassionate into someone who was indifferent to suffering — of turning someone, in that particular moment, into a different person. Epidemics are, at their root, about this very process of transformation. When we are trying to make an idea or attitude or product tip, we're trying to change our audience in some small yet critical respect: we're trying to infect them, sweep them up in our epidemic, convert them from hostility to acceptance. That can be done through the influence of special kinds of people, people of extraordinary personal connection. That's the Law of the Few. It can be done by changing the content of communication, by making a message so memorable that it sticks in someone's mind and compels them to action. That is the Stickiness Factor. I think that both of those laws make intuitive sense. But we need to remember that small changes in context can be just as important in tipping epidemics, even though that fact appears to violate some of our most deeply held assumptions about human nature.

This does not mean that our inner psychological states and personal histories are not important in explaining our behavior. An enormous percentage of those who engage in violent acts, for example, have some kind of psychiatric disorder or come from deeply disturbed backgrounds. But there is a world of difference between being inclined toward violence and actually committing a violent act. A crime is a relatively rare and aberrant event. For a crime to be committed, something extra, something additional, has to happen to tip a troubled person toward violence, and what the Power of Context is saying is that those Tipping Points may be as simple and trivial as everyday signs of disorder like graffiti and fare-beating. The implications of this idea are enormous. The previous notion that disposition is everything — that the cause of violent behavior is always "sociopathic personality" or "deficient superego" or the inability to delay gratification or some evil in the genes — is, in the end, the most passive and reactive of ideas about crime. It says that once you catch a criminal you can try to help him get better — give him Prozac, put him in therapy, try to rehabilitate him — but there is very little you can do to prevent crime from happening in the first place. The old understanding of handling crime epidemics leads inevitably to a preoccupation with defensive measures against crime. Put an extra lock on the door, to slow the burglar down and maybe encourage him to go next door. Lock up criminals for longer, so that they have less opportunity to do the rest of us harm. Move to the suburbs, to put as much distance as possible between yourself and the majority of criminals.

Once you understand that context matters, however, that specific and relatively small elements in the environment can serve as Tipping Points, that defeatism is turned upside down. Environmental Tipping Points are things that we can change: we can fix broken windows and clean up graffiti and change the signals that invite crime in the first place. Crime can be more than understood. It can be prevented. There is a broader dimension to this. Judith Harris has convincingly argued that peer influence and community influence are more important than family influence in determining how children turn out. Studies of juvenile delinquency and high school drop-out rates, for example, demonstrate that a child is better off in a good neighborhood and a troubled family than he or she is in a troubled neighborhood and a good family. We spend so much time celebrating the importance and power of family influence that it may seem, at first blush, that this can't be true. But in reality it is no more than an obvious and commonsensical extension of the Power of Context, because it says simply that children are powerfully shaped by their external environment, that the features of our immediate social and physical world — the streets we walk down, the people we encounter — play a huge role in shaping who we are and how we act. It isn't just serious criminal behavior, in the end, that is sensitive to environmental cues, it is all behavior. Weird as it sounds, if you add up the meaning of the Stanford prison experiment and the New York subway experiment, they suggest that it is possible to be a better person on a clean street or in a clean subway than in one littered with trash and graffiti.

"In a situation like this, you're in a combat situation," Goetz told his neighbor Myra Friedman, in an anguished telephone call just days after the shooting. "You're not thinking in a normal way. Your memory isn't even working normally. You are so hyped up. Your vision actually changes. Your field of view changes. Your capabilities change. What you are capable of changes." He acted, Goetz went on, "viciously and savagely. . . . If you corner a rat and you are about to butcher it, okay? The way I responded was viciously and savagely, just like that, like a rat."

Of course he did. He was in a rat hole.

FIVE

The Power of Context (Part Two)

THE MAGIC NUMBER ONE HUNDRED AND FIFTY

I n 1996, a sometime actress and playwright by the name of Rebecca Wells published a book entitled *Divine Secrets of the Ya-Ya Sisterhood*. Its arrival in the bookstores was not a major literary event. Wells had written one previous book — *Little Altars Everywhere* — which had been a minor cult hit in and around her hometown of Seattle. But she was not Danielle Steel or Mary Higgins Clark. When Wells gave a reading soon after her book was published in Greenwich, Connecticut, there were seven people in the audience. She had a smattering of reviews here and there, mostly positive, and in the end her book sold a very respectable 15,000 copies in hardcover.

A year later, *Ya-Ya Sisterhood* came out in paperback. The first edition of 18,000 copies sold out in the first few months, exceeding expectations. By early summer, total paperback sales had reached 30,000, and both Wells and her editor began to get the sense that something strange and wonderful was about to happen. "I'd be signing books and there would be groups of women who would come together — six or seven women — and they would have me sign anywhere between three and ten books," Wells remembered later. Wells's editor, Diane Reverand, went to her marketing people and said it was time for an advertising campaign. They bought one ad, opposite the contents page of the *New Yorker* magazine, and in the space of a month sales doubled to 60,000. Going from one reading to the next, across the country, Wells began to see changes in the composition of her audience. "I started noticing mothers and daughters coming. The daughters would be in their late thirties, early forties. The mothers were of the generation who went to high school during World War Two. Then I noticed that there started to be three generations coming, twentysomethings as well. And then, to my total delight — and this didn't happen until later — there would be teenagers and fifth-graders."

Divine Secrets of the Ya-Ya Sisterhood was not yet on the bestseller lists. That wouldn't happen until February 1998, when it would hit the charts and stay there, through 48 printings and 2.5 million copies. The national media attention — the articles in the big women's magazines and the appearance on television shows that would turn Wells into a celebrity — hadn't started yet either. But through the power of word of mouth, her book had tipped. "The turning point for me was probably in northern California, the winter after the paperback came out," Wells said. "I walked into a situation where all of a sudden there were seven hundred and eight hundred people at my readings."

Why did *Ya-Ya Sisterhood* turn into an epidemic? In retrospect, the answer seems fairly straightforward. The book itself is heartwarming and beautifully written, a compelling story of friendship and mother-daughter relationships. It spoke to people. It's sticky. Then there's the fact that Wells herself is an actress. She didn't read from her novel as she traveled across the country so much as she acted it out, playing each character with such skill that she turned her readings into performances. Wells is a classic Salesman. But there is a third, less obvious, factor here, which has to do with the last of the principles of epidemics. The success of *Ya-Ya* is a tribute to the Power of Context. More specifically, it is testimony to the power of one specific aspect of context, which is the critical role that groups play in social epidemics.

1.

In a way, this is an obvious observation. Anyone who has ever been to the movies knows that the size of the crowd in the theater has a big effect on how good the movie seems: comedies are never funnier and thrillers never more thrilling than in a packed movie house. Psychologists tell us much the same thing: that when people are asked to consider evidence or make decisions in a group, they come to very different conclusions than when they are asked the same questions by themselves. Once we're part of a group, we're all susceptible to peer pressure and social norms and any number of other kinds of influence that can play a critical role in sweeping us up in the beginnings of an epidemic.

Have you ever wondered, for example, how religious movements get started? Usually, we think of them as a product of highly charismatic evangelists, people like the Apostle Paul or Billy Graham or Brigham Young. But the spread of any new and contagious ideology also has a lot to do with the skillful use of group power. In the late eighteenth and early nineteenth centuries, for example, the Methodist movement became epidemic in England and North America, tipping from 20,000 to 90,000 followers in the U.S. in the space of five or six years in the 1780s. But Methodism's founder, John Wesley, was by no means the most charismatic preacher of his era. That honor belonged to George Whitfield, an orator of such power and charisma that, it was said, he once charmed a five-pound contribution out of Benjamin Franklin — who was, of course, the furthest thing from a churchgoer. Nor was Wesley a great theologian, in the tradition of, say, John Calvin or Martin Luther. His genius was organizational. Wesley would travel around England and North America delivering open-air sermons to thousands of people. But he didn't just preach. He also stayed long enough in each town to form the most enthusiastic of his converts into religious societies, which in turn he subdivided into smaller classes of a dozen or so people. Converts were required to attend weekly meetings and to adhere to a strict code of conduct. If they failed to live up to Methodist standards, they were expelled from the group. This was a group, in other words, that stood for something. Over the course of his life, Wesley traveled ceaselessly among these groups, covering as much as four thousand miles a year by horseback, reinforcing the tenets of Methodist belief. He was a classic Connector. He was a super Paul Revere. The difference is, though, that he wasn't one person with ties to many other people. He was one person with ties to many groups, which is a small but critical distinction. Wesley realized that if you wanted to bring about a fundamental change in people's belief and behavior, a change that would persist and serve as an example to others, you needed to create a community around them, where those new beliefs could be practiced and expressed and nurtured.

This, I think, helps to explain why the *Ya-Ya Sisterhood* tipped as well. The first bestseller list on which *Ya-Ya Sisterhood* appeared was the Northern California Independent Bookseller's list. Northern California, as Wells said, was where 700 and 800 people first began showing up at her readings. It was where the *Ya-Ya* epidemic began. Why? Because, according to Reverand, the San Francisco area is home to one of the country's strongest book-group cultures, and from the beginning *Ya-Ya* was what publishers refer to as a "book-group book." It was the kind of emotionally sophisticated, character-driven, multi-layered novel that invites reflection and discussion, and book groups were flocking to it. The groups of women who were coming to Wells's readings were members of reading groups, and they were buying extra copies not just for family and friends but for other members of their group. And because *Ya-Ya* was being talked about and read in groups, the book itself became that much stickier. It's easier to remember and appreciate something, after all, if you discuss it for two hours with your best friends. It becomes a social experience, an object of conversation.

Ya-Ya's roots in book-group culture tipped it into a larger word-of-mouth epidemic.

Wells says that at the end of readings, during the question-and-answer session, women in the audience would tell her, "We've been in a book group for two years, and then we read your book and something else happened. It started to drop down to a level of sharing that was more like friendship. They told me that they had started going to the beach together, or having parties at each other's houses." Women began forming Ya-Ya Sisterhood groups of their own, in imitation of the group described in the book, and bringing Wells pictures of their group for her to sign. Wesley's Methodism spread like wildfire through England and America because Wesley was shuttling back and forth among hundreds and hundreds of groups, and each group was then taking his message and making it even stickier. The word about *Ya-Ya* was spreading in the same way, from reading group to reading group, from Ya-Ya group to Ya-Ya group and from one of Wells's readings to another, because for over a year she stopped everything else and toured the country nonstop.

The lesson of *Ya-Ya* and John Wesley is that small, close-knit groups have the power to magnify the epidemic potential of a message or idea. That conclusion, however, still leaves a number of critical questions unanswered. The word *group,* for instance, is a term used to describe everything from a basketball team to the Teamsters Union, from two couples on a holiday to the Republican Party. If we are interested in starting an epidemic — in reaching a Tipping Point — what are the most effective kinds of groups? Is there a simple rule of thumb that distinguishes a group with real social social authority from a group with little power at all? As it turns out, there is. It's called the Rule of 150, and it is a fascinating example of the strange and unexpected ways in which context affects the course of social epidemics.

2.

There is a concept in cognitive psychology called the channel capacity, which refers to the amount of space in our brain for certain kinds of information. Suppose, for example, that I played you a number of different musical tones, at random, and asked you to identify each one with a number. If I played you a really low tone, you would call it one, and if I played you a medium tone you would call it two, and a high tone you would call three. The purpose of the test is to find out how long you can continue to distinguish among different tones. People with perfect pitch, of course, can play this game forever. You can play them dozens of tones, and they'll be able to distinguish between all of them. But for the majority of us, this game is much harder. Most people can divide tones into only about six different categories before they begin to make mistakes and start lumping different tones in the same category. This is a remarkably consistent finding. If, for example, I played you five very high pitched tones, you'd be able to tell them apart. And if I played you five very low pitched tones, you'd be able to tell them apart. You'd think, then, that if I combined those high and low tones and played them for you all at once, you'd be able to divide them into ten categories. But you won't be able to. Chances are you'll still be stuck at about six categories.

This natural limit shows up again and again in simple tests. If I make you drink twenty glasses of iced tea, each with a different amount of sugar in it, and ask you to sort them into categories according to sweetness, you'll only be able to divide them into six or seven different categories before you begin to make mistakes. Or if I flash dots on a screen in front of you very quickly and ask you to count how many you see, you'd get the number right up to about seven dots, and then you'd need to guess. "There seems to be some limitation built into us either by learning or by the design of our nervous systems, a limit that keeps our channel capacities in this general range," the psychologist George Miller concluded in his famous essay "The Magical Number Seven." This is the reason that telephone numbers have seven digits. "Bell wanted a number to be as long as possible so they could have as large a capacity as possible, but not so long that people couldn't remember it," says Jonathan Cohen, a memory researcher at Princeton University. At eight or nine digits, the local telephone number would exceed the human channel capacity: there would be many more wrong numbers.

As human beings, in other words, we can only handle so much information at once. Once we pass a certain boundary, we become overwhelmed. What I'm describing here is an intellectual capacity — our ability to process raw information. But if you think about it, we clearly have a channel capacity for feelings as well.

Take a minute, for example, to make a list of all the people you know whose death would leave you truly devastated. Chances are you will come up with around 12 names. That, at least, is the average answer that most people give to that question. Those names make up what psychologists call our sympathy group. Why aren't groups any larger? Partly it's a question of time. If you look at the names on your sympathy list, they are probably the people whom you devote the most attention to — either on the telephone, in person, or thinking and worrying about. If your list was twice as long, if it had 30 names on it, and, as a result, you spent only half as much time with everyone on it, would you still be as close to everyone? Probably not. To be someone's best friend requires a minimum investment of time. More than that, though, it takes emotional energy. Caring about someone deeply is exhausting. At a certain point, at somewhere between 10 and 15 people, we begin to overload, just as we begin to overload when we have to distinguish between too many tones. It's a function of the way humans are constructed. As the evolutionary biologist S. L. Washburn writes:

> Most of human evolution took place before the advent of agriculture when men lived in small groups, on a face-to-face basis. As a result human biology has evolved as an adaptive mechanism to conditions that have largely ceased to exist. Man evolved to feel strongly about few people, short distances, and relatively brief intervals of time; and these are still the dimensions of life that are important to him.

Perhaps the most interesting natural limit, however, is what might be called our social channel capacity. The case for a social capacity has been made, most persuasively, by the British anthropologist Robin Dunbar. Dunbar begins with a simple observation. Primates — monkeys, chimps, baboons, humans — have the biggest brains of all mammals. More important, a specific part of the brain of humans and other primates — the region known as the neocortex, which deals with complex thought and reasoning — is huge by mammal standards. For years, scientists have argued back and forth about why this is the case. One theory is that our brains evolved because our primate ancestors began to engage in more sophisticated food gathering: instead of just eating grasses and leaves they began eating fruit, which takes more thinking power. You travel much farther to find fruit than leaves, so you need to be able to create mental maps. You have to worry about ripeness. You have to peel parts away in order to eat the flesh of a fruit, and so on. The problem with that theory is that if you try to match up brain size with eating patterns among primates, it doesn't work. There are primate leaf-eaters with big brains and fruit-eaters with smaller brains, just as there are primates with small cortexes who travel great distances for their food and primates with big brains who stay at home to eat, so the food argument is a dead end. So what does correlate with brain size? The answer, Dunbar argues, is group size. If you look at any species of primate — at every variety of monkey and ape — the larger their neocortex is, the larger the average size of the groups they live with.

Dunbar's argument is that brains evolve, they get bigger, in order to handle the complexities of larger social groups. If you belong to a group of five people, Dunbar points out, you have to keep track of ten separate relationships: your relationships with the four others in your circle and the six other two-way relationships between the others.

That's what it means to know everyone in the circle. You have to understand the personal dynamics of the group, juggle different personalities, keep people happy, manage the demands on your own time and attention, and so on. If you belong to a group of twenty people, however, there are now 190 two-way relationships to keep track of: 19 involving yourself and 171 involving the rest of the group. That's a fivefold increase in the size of the group, but a twentyfold increase in the amount of information processing needed to "know" the other members of the group. Even a relatively small increase in the size of a group, in other words, creates a significant additional social and intellectual burden.

Humans socialize in the largest groups of all primates because we are the only animals with brains large enough to handle the complexities of that social arrangement. Dunbar has actually developed an equation, which works for most primates, in which he plugs in what he calls the neocortex ratio of a particular species — the size of the neocortex relative to the size of the brain — and the equation spits out the expected maximum group size of the animal. If you plug in the neocortex ratio for Homo sapiens, you get a group estimate of 147.8 — or roughly 150. "The figure of 150 seems to represent the maximum number of individuals with whom we can have a genuinely social relationship, the kind of relationship that goes with knowing who they are and how they relate to us. Putting it another way, it's the number of people you would not feel embarrassed about joining uninvited for a drink if you happened to bump into them in a bar."

Dunbar has combed through the anthropological literature and found that the number 150 pops up again and again. For example, he looks at 21 different hunter-gatherer societies for which we have solid historical evidence, from the Walbiri of Australia to the Tauade of New Guinea to the Ammassalik of Greenland to the Ona of Tierra del Fuego and found that the average number of people in their villages was 148.4. The same pattern holds true for military organization. "Over the years military planners have arrived at a rule of thumb which dictates that functional fighting units cannot be substantially larger than 200 men," Dunbar writes. "This, I suspect, is not simply a matter of how the generals in the rear exercise control and coordination, because companies have remained obdurately stuck at this size despite all the advances in communications technology since the first world war. Rather, it is as though the planners have discovered, by trial and error over the centuries, that it is hard to get more than this number of men sufficiently familiar with each other so that they can work together as a functional unit." It is still possible, of course, to run an army with larger groups. But at a bigger size you have to impose complicated hierarchies and rules and regulations and formal measures to try to command loyalty and cohesion. But below 150, Dunbar argues, it is possible to achieve these same goals informally: "At this size, orders can be implemented and unruly behavior controlled on the basis of personal loyalties and direct man-to-man contacts. With larger groups, this becomes impossible."

Then there is the example of the religious group known as the Hutterites, who for hundreds of years have lived in self-sufficient agricultural colonies in Europe and, since the early twentieth century, in North America. The Hutterites (who came out of the same tradition as the Amish and the Mennonites) have a strict policy that every time a colony approaches 150, they split it in two and start a new one. "Keeping things under 150 just seems to be the best and most efficient way to manage a group of people," Bill Gross, one of the leaders of a Hutterite colony outside Spokane told me. "When things get larger than that, people become strangers to one another." The Hutterites, obviously, didn't get this idea from contemporary evolutionary psychology. They've been following the 150 rule for centuries. But their rationale fits perfectly with Dunbar's theories. At 150, the Hutterites believe, something happens — something indefinable but very real — that somehow changes the nature of community overnight. "In smaller groups people are a lot closer. They're knit together, which is very important if you want to be effective and successful at community life," Gross said. "If you get too large, you don't have enough work in common. You don't have enough things in common, and then you start to become strangers and that close-knit fellowship starts to get lost." Gross spoke from experience. He had been in Hutterite colonies that had come near to that magic number and seen firsthand how things had changed. "What happens when you get that big is that the group starts, just on its own, to form a sort of clan." He made a gesture with his hands, as if to demonstrate division. "You get two or three groups within the larger group. That is something you really try to prevent, and when it happens it is a good time to branch out."

3.

We have seen, in this book, how a number of relatively minor changes in our external environment can have a dramatic effect on how we behave and who we are. Clean up graffiti and all of a sudden people who would otherwise commit crimes suddenly don't. Tell a seminarian that he has to hurry and all of a sudden he starts to ignore bystanders in obvious distress. The Rule of 150 suggests that the size of a group is another one of those subtle contextual factors that can make a big difference. In the case of the Hutterites, people who are willing to go along with the group, who can be easily infected with the community ethos below the level of 150, somehow, suddenly — with just the smallest change in the size of the community — become divided and alienated. Once that line, that Tipping Point, is crossed, they begin to behave very differently.

If we want groups to serve as incubators for contagious messages, then, as they did in the case of *Divine Secrets of the Ya-Ya Sisterhood* or the early Methodist church, we have to keep groups below the 150 Tipping Point. Above that point, there begin to be structural impediments to the ability of the group to agree and act with one voice. If we want to, say, develop schools in disadvantaged communities that can successfully counteract the poisonous atmosphere of their surrounding neighborhoods, this tells us that we're probably better off building lots of little schools than one or two big ones. The Rule of 150 says that congregants of a rapidly expanding church, or the members of a social club, or anyone in a group activity banking on the epidemic spread of shared ideals needs to be particularly cognizant of the perils of bigness. Crossing the 150 line is a small change that can make a big difference.

Perhaps the best example of an organization that has successfully navigated this problem is Gore Associates, a privately held, multimillion-dollar high-tech firm based in Newark, Delaware. Gore is the company that makes the water-resistant Gore-Tex fabric, as well as Glide dental floss, special insulating coatings for computer cables, and a variety of sophisticated specialty cartridges, filter bags, and tubes for the automobile, semiconductor, pharmaceutical, and medical industries. At Gore there are no titles. If you ask people who work there for their card, it will just say their name and underneath it the word "Associate," regardless of how much money they make or how much responsibility they have or how long they have been at the company. People don't have bosses, they have sponsors — mentors — who watch out for their interests. There are no organization charts, no budgets, no elaborate strategic plans. Salaries are determined collectively. Headquarters for the company is a low-slung, unpretentious red brick building. The "executive" offices are small, plainly furnished rooms, along a narrow corridor. The corners of Gore buildings tend to be conference rooms or free space, so that no one can be said to have a more prestigious office. When I visited a Gore associate named Bob Hen, at one of the company's plants in Delaware, I tried, unsuccessfully, to get him to tell me what his position was. I suspected, from the fact that he had been recommended to me, that he was one of the top executives. But his office wasn't any bigger than anyone else's. His card just called him an "associate." He didn't seem to have a secretary, one that I could see anyway. He wasn't dressed any differently from anyone else, and when I kept asking the question again and again, all he finally said, with a big grin, was, "I'm a meddler."

Gore is, in short, a very unusual company with a clear and well-articulated philosophy. It is a big established company attempting to behave like a small entrepreneurial start-up. By all accounts, that attempt has been wildly successful. Whenever business experts make lists of the best American companies to work for, or whenever consultants give speeches on the best-managed American companies, Gore is on the list. It has a rate of employee turnover that is about a third the industry average. It has been profitable for thirty-five consecutive years and has growth rates and an innovative, high-profit product line that is the envy of the industry. Gore has managed to create a small-company ethos so infectious and sticky that it has survived their growth into a billion-dollar company with thousands of employees. And how did they do that? By (among other things) adhering to the Rule of 150.

Wilbert "Bill" Gore — the late founder of the company — was no more influenced, of course, by the ideas of Robin Dunbar than the Hutterites were. Like them, he seems to have stumbled on the principle by trial and error. "We found again and again that things get clumsy at a hundred and fifty," he told an interviewer some years ago, so 150 employees per plant became the company goal. In the electronics division of the company, that means that no plant was built larger than 50,000 square feet, since there was almost no way to put many more than 150 people in a building that size. "People used to ask me, how do you do your long-term planning," Hen said. "And I'd say, that's easy, we put a hundred and fifty parking spaces in the lot, and when people start parking on the grass, we know it's time to build a new plant." That new plant doesn't have to be far away. In Gore's home state of Delaware, for instance, the company has three plants within sight of each other. In fact, the company has fifteen plants within a twelve-mile radius in Delaware and Maryland. The buildings only have to be distinct enough to allow for an individual culture in each. "We've found that a parking lot is a big gap between buildings," one longtime associate, Burt Chase, told me. "You've got to pick yourself up and walk across the lot, and that's a big effort. That's almost as much effort as it takes to get in your car and drive five miles. There's a lot of independence in just having a separate building." As Gore has grown in recent years, the company has undergone an almost constant process of division and redivision. Other companies would just keep adding additions to the main plant, or extend a production line, or double shifts. Gore tries to split up groups into smaller and smaller pieces. When I visited Gore, for example, they had just divided their Gore-Tex apparel business into two groups, in order to get under the 150 limit. The more fashion-oriented consumer business of boots and backpacks and hiking gear was going off on its own, leaving behind the institutional business that makes Gore-Tex uniforms for firefighters and soldiers.

It's not hard to see the connection between this kind of organizational structure and the unusual, free-form management style of Gore. The kind of bond that Dunbar describes in small groups is essentially a kind of peer pressure: it's knowing people well enough that what they think of you matters. He said, remember, that the company is the basic unit of military organization because, in a group under 150, "orders can be implemented and unruly behavior controlled on the basis of personal loyalties and direct man-to-man contacts." That's what Bill Gross was saying about his Hutterite community as well. The fissures they see in Hutterite colonies that grow too big are the fissures that result when the bonds among some commune members begin to weaken. Gore doesn't need formal management structures in its small plants — it doesn't need the usual layers of middle and upper management — because in groups that small, informal personal relationships are more effective. "The pressure that comes to bear if we are not efficient at a plant, if we are not creating good earnings for the company, the peer pressure is unbelievable," Jim Buckley, a longtime associate of the firm, told me. "This is what you get when you have small teams, where everybody knows everybody. Peer pressure is much more powerful than a concept of a boss. Many, many times more powerful. People want to live up to what is expected of them." In a larger, conventional-sized manufacturing plant, Buckley said, you might get the same kind of pressures. But they would work only within certain parts of the plant. The advantage of a Gore plant is that every part of the process for designing and making and marketing a given product is subject to the same group scrutiny. "I just came back from Lucent Technologies up in New Jersey," Buckley told me. "It's the plant where they make cells that operate our cellular phones — the pods, the boxes up and down I-95 that carry the signals. I spent a day in their plant. They have six hundred and fifty people. At best, their manufacturing people know some of their design people. But that's it. They don't know any of the sales-people. They don't know the sales-support people. They don't know the R and D people. They don't know any of these people, nor do they know what is going on in those other aspects of the business. The pressure I'm talking about is the kind you get when salespeople are in the same world as the manufacturing people, and the salesperson who wants to get a customer order taken care of can go directly and talk to someone they know on the manufac-turing team and say, I need that order. Here's two people. One is trying to make the product, one is trying to get the product out. They go head to head and talk about it. That's peer pressure. You don't see that at Lucent. They are removed. In the manufacturing realm, they had a hundred and fifty people, and they worked closely together and there was peer pressure about how to be the best and how to be the most innovative. But it just didn't go outside the group. They don't know each other. You go into the cafe-teria and there are little groups of people. It's a different kind of experience."

What Buckley is referring to here is the benefit of unity, of having everyone in a complex enterprise share a common relationship. There is a useful concept in psy-chology that, I think, makes it much clearer what he's speaking about. This is what University of Virginia psy-chologist Daniel Wegner calls "transactive memory." When we talk about memory, we aren't just talking about ideas and impressions and facts stored inside our heads.

An awful lot of what we remember is actually stored outside our brains. Most of us deliberately don't memorize most of the phone numbers we need. But we do memorize where to find them — in a phone book, or in our personal Rolodex. Or we memorize the number 411, so we can call directory assistance. Nor do most of us know, say, the capital of Paraguay or some other obscure country. Why bother? It's an awful lot easier to buy an atlas and store that kind of information there. Perhaps most important, though, we store information with other people. Couples do this automatically. A few years ago, for example, Wegner set up a memory test with 59 couples, all of whom had been dating for at least three months. Half of the couples were allowed to stay together, and half were split up, and given a new partner whom they didn't know. Wegner then asked all the pairs to read 64 statements, each with an underlined word, like "Midori is a Japanese melon *liqueur.*" Five minutes after looking at all the statements, the pairs were asked to write down as many as they could remember. Sure enough, the pairs who knew each other remembered substantially more items than those who didn't know each other. Wegner argues that when people know each other well, they create an implicit joint memory system — a transactive memory system — which is based on an understanding about who is best suited to remember what kinds of things. "Relationship development is often understood as a process of mutual self-disclosure," he writes. "Although it is probably more romantic to cast this process as one of interpersonal revelation and acceptance, it can also be appreciated as a necessary precursor to transactive memory." Transactive memory is part of what intimacy means. In fact, Wegner argues, it is the loss of this kind of joint memory that helps to make divorce so painful. "Divorced people who suffer depression and complain of cognitive dysfunction may be expressing the loss of their external memory systems," he writes. "They once were able to discuss their experiences to reach a shared understanding.... They once could count on access to a wide range of storage in their partner, and this, too, is gone.... The loss of transactive memory feels like losing a part of one's own mind."

In a family, this process of memory sharing is even more pronounced. Most of us remember, at one time, only a fraction of the day-to-day details and histories of our family life. But we know, implicitly, where to go to find the answers to our questions — whether it is up to our spouse to remember where we put our keys or our thirteen-year-old to find out how to work the computer or our mother to find out details of our childhood. Perhaps more important, when new information arises, we know who should have responsibility for storing it. This is how, in a family, expertise emerges. The thirteen-year-old is the family expert on the computer not just because he has the greatest aptitude for electronic equipment or because he uses computers the most, but also because when new information about the family computer arises, he is the one assigned, automatically, to remember it. Expertise leads to more expertise. Why bother remembering how to install software if your son, close at hand, can do it for you? Since mental energy is limited, we concentrate on what we do best. Women tend to be the "experts" in child care, even in modern, dual-career families, because their initial greater involvement in raising a baby leads them to be relied on more than the man in storing child-care information, and then that initial expertise leads them to be relied on even more for child-care matters, until — often unintentionally — the woman shoulders the bulk of the intellectual responsibility for the child. "When each person has group-acknowledged responsibility for particular tasks and facts, greater efficiency is inevitable," Wegner says. "Each domain is handled by the fewest capable of doing so, and responsibility for the domains is continuous over time rather than intermittently assigned by circumstance."

When Jim Buckley says, then, that working at Gore is a "different kind of experience," what he is talking about, in part, is that Gore has a highly effective institutional transactive memory. Here, for example, is how one Gore associate describes the kind of "knowing" that emerges in a small plant: "It's not just do you know somebody. It's do you really know them well enough that you know their skills and abilities and passions. That's what you like, what you do, what you want to do, what you are truly good at. Not, are you a nice person." What that associate is talking about is the psychological preconditions for transactive memory: it's knowing someone well enough to know what they know, and knowing them well enough so that you can trust them to know things in their specialty. It's the re-creation, on an organization-wide level, of the kind of intimacy and trust that exists in a family.

Now, of course, if you have a company that is making paper towels or stamping out nuts and bolts, you might not care. Not every company needs this degree of connectedness. But in a high-technology company like Gore, which relies for its market edge on its ability to innovate and react quickly to demanding and sophisticated customers, this kind of global memory system is critical. It makes the company incredibly efficient. It means that cooperation is easier. It means that you move much faster to get things done or create teams of workers or find out an answer to a problem. It means that people in one part of the company can get access to the impressions and expertise of people in a completely different part of the company. At Lucent, the 150 people in manufacturing may have their own memory network. But how much more effective would the company be if, like Gore, everyone in the plant was part of the same transactive system — if R&D was hooked into design and design into manufacturing and manufacturing into sales? "One of the immediate reactions we get when we talk to people is 'Man, your system sounds chaotic. How in the devil can you do anything with no obvious authority?' But it's not chaos. It isn't a problem," Burt Chase said. "It's hard to appreciate that unless you are working in it. It's the advantage of understanding people's strengths. It's knowing — where can I get my best advice? And if you have some knowledge about people, you can do that."

What Gore has created, in short, is an organized mechanism that makes it far easier for new ideas and information moving around the organization to tip — to go from one person or one part of the group to the entire group all at once. That's the advantage of adhering to the Rule of 150. You can exploit the bonds of memory and peer pressure. Were Gore to try to reach each employee singly, their task would have been much harder, just as Rebecca Wells's task would have been much harder if her readers came to her readings not in groups of six and seven but by themselves. And had Gore tried to put everyone in one big room, it wouldn't have worked either. In order to be unified — in order to spread a specific, company ideology to all of its employees — Gore had to break itself up into semi-autonomous small pieces. That is the paradox of the epidemic: that in order to create one contagious movement, you often have to create many small movements first. Rebecca Wells says that what she began to realize as the *Ya-Ya* epidemic grew was that it wasn't really about her or even about her book: it wasn't one epidemic focused on one thing. It was thousands of different epidemics, all focused on the groups that had grown up around *Ya-Ya*. "I began to realize," she said, "that these women had built their own Ya-Ya relationships, not so much to the book but to each other."

SIX

Case Study

RUMORS, SNEAKERS, AND
THE POWER OF TRANSLATION

irwalking is the name given to the skateboarding move in which the skater takes off from a
ramp, slips his board out from under his feet,
and then takes one or two long, exaggerated
strides in the air before landing. It is a classic stunt, a staple
of traditional skateboarding, which is why when two
entrepreneurs decided in the mid-1980s to start manufacturing athletic shoes aimed at hard-core skateboarders,
they called the company Airwalk. Airwalk was based outside San Diego and rooted in the teenage beach-and-skate
culture of the region. In the beginning, the firm made a
canvas shoe in wild colors and prints that became a kind
of alternative fashion statement. They also made a technical skate shoe in suede, with a thick sole and a heavily
cushioned upper that — at least at first — was almost as
stiff as the skateboard itself. But the skaters became so
devoted to the product that they would wash the shoes
over and again, then drive over them in cars to break them

in. Airwalk was cool. It sponsored professional skateboarders, and developed a cult following at the skate
events, and after a few years had built up a comfortable
$13 million-a-year business.

Companies can continue at that level indefinitely, in a
state of low-level equilibrium, serving a small but loyal
audience. But the owners of Airwalk wanted more. They
wanted to build themselves into an international brand,
and in the early 1990s they changed course. They reorga-
nized their business operations. They redesigned their
shoes. They expanded their focus to include not just skateboarding but also surfing, snowboarding, mountain biking,
and bicycle racing, sponsoring riders in all of those sports
and making Airwalk synonymous with the active, alternative lifestyle. They embarked on an aggressive grassroots
campaign to meet the buyers for youth-oriented shoe
stores. They persuaded Foot Locker to try them out on an
experimental basis. They worked to get alternative rock
bands to wear their shoes on stage and, perhaps most
important, they decided to hire a small advertising agency
named Lambesis to rethink their marketing campaign.
Under Lambesis's direction, Airwalk exploded. In 1993, it
had been a $16 million company. In 1994, it had sales of $44
million. In 1995, sales jumped to $150 million, and the year
after that they hit $175 million. At its peak, Airwalk was
ranked by one major marketing research company as the
thirteenth "coolest" brand among teenagers in the world,
and the number three footwear brand, behind Nike and
Adidas. Somehow, within the space of a year or two, Airwalk was jolted out of its quiet equilibrium on the beaches
of southern California. In the mid-1990s, Airwalk tipped.

The Tipping Point has been concerned so far with defining epidemics and explaining the principles of epidemic transmission. The experiences of Paul Revere and *Sesame Street* and crime in New York City and Gore Associates each illustrate one of the rules of Tipping Points. In everyday life, however, the problems and situations we face don't always embody the principles of epidemics so neatly. In this section of the book, I'd like to look at less straight-forward problems, and see how the idea of Mavens and Connectors and Stickiness and Context — either singly or in combination — helps to explain them.

Why, for example, did Airwalk tip? The short answer is that Lambesis came up with an inspired advertising campaign. At the start, working with only a small budget, the creative director of Lambesis, Chad Farmer, came up with a series of dramatic images — single photographs showing the Airwalk user relating to his shoes in some weird way. In one, a young man is wearing an Airwalk shoe on his head, with the laces hanging down like braids, as his laces are being cut by a barber. In another, a leather-clad girl is holding up a shiny vinyl Airwalk shoe like a mirror and using it to apply lipstick. The ads were put on billboards and in "wild postings" on construction-site walls and in alternative magazines. As Airwalk grew, Lambesis went into television. In one of the early Airwalk commercials, the camera pans across a bedroom floor littered with discarded clothing. It then settles under the bed, as the air is filled with grunting and puffing and noise of the bedsprings going up and down. Finally the camera comes out from under the bed and we see a young, slightly dazed-looking youth, holding an Airwalk shoe in his hand, jumping up and down on his bed as he tries unsuccessfully to kill a spider on the ceiling. The ads were entirely visual, designed to appeal to youth all over the world. They were rich in detail and visually arresting. They all featured a truculent, slightly geeky anti-hero. And they were funny, in a sophisticated way. This was great advertising; in the years since the first Airwalk ads appeared, the look and feel of that campaign has been copied again and again by other companies trying to be "cool." The strength of the Lambesis campaign was in more than the look of their work, though. Airwalk tipped because its advertising was founded very explicitly on the principles of epidemic transmission.

1.

Perhaps the best way to understand what Lambesis did is to go back to what sociologists call the diffusion model, which is a detailed, academic way of looking at how a contagious idea or product or innovation moves through a population. One of the most famous diffusion studies is Bruce Ryan and Neal Gross's analysis of the spread of hybrid seed corn in Greene County, Iowa, in the 1930s. The new corn seed was introduced in Iowa in 1928, and it was superior in every respect to the seed that had been used by farmers for decades before. But it wasn't adopted all at once. Of the 259 farmers studied by Ryan and Gross, only a handful had started planting the new seed by 1932 and 1933. In 1934, 16 took the plunge. In 1935, 21 followed, then 36, and the year after that a whopping 61 and then 46, 36, 14, and 3, until by 1941, all but two of the 259 farmers studied were using the new seeds. In the language of diffusion research, the handful of farmers who started trying hybrid seed at the very beginning of the 1930s were the Innovators, the adventurous ones. The slightly larger group who were infected by them were the Early Adopters. They were the opinion leaders in the community, the respected, thoughtful people who watched and analyzed what those wild Innovators were doing and then followed suit. Then came the big bulge of farmers in 1936, 1937, and 1938, the Early Majority and the Late Majority, the deliberate and the skeptical mass, who would never try anything until the most respected of farmers had tried it first. They caught the seed virus and passed it on, finally, to the Laggards, the most traditional of all, who see no urgent reason to change. If you plot that progression on a graph, it forms a perfect epidemic curve — starting slowly, tipping just as the Early Adopters start using the seed, then rising sharply as the Majority catches on, and falling away at the end when the Laggards come straggling in.

The message here — new seeds — was highly contagious and powerfully sticky. A farmer, after all, could see with his own eyes, from spring planting to fall harvest, how much better the new seeds were than the old. It's hard to imagine how that particular innovation *couldn't* have tipped. But in many cases the contagious spread of a new idea is actually quite tricky.

The business consultant Geoffrey Moore, for example, uses the example of high technology to argue that there is a substantial difference between the people who originate trends and ideas and the people in the Majority who eventually take them up. These two groups may be next to each other on the word-of-mouth continuum. But they don't communicate particularly well. The first two groups — the Innovators and Early Adopters — are visionaries. They want revolutionary change, something that sets them apart qualitatively from their competitors. They are the people who buy brand-new technology, before it's been perfected or proved or before the price has come down. They have small companies. They are just starting out. They are willing to take enormous risks. The Early Majority, by contrast, are big companies. They have to worry about any change fitting into their complex arrangement of suppliers and distributors. "If the goal of visionaries is to make a quantum leap forward, the goal of pragmatists is to make a percentage improvement — incremental, measurable, predictable progress," Moore writes. "If they are installing a new product, they want to know how other people have fared with it. The word risk is a negative word in their vocabulary — it does not connote opportunity or excitement but rather the chance to waste money and time. They will undertake risks when required, but they first will put in place safety nets and manage the risks very closely."

Moore's argument is that the attitude of the Early Adopters and the attitude of the Early Majority are fundamentally incompatible. Innovations don't just slide effortlessly from one group to the next. There is a chasm between them. All kinds of high-tech products fail, never making it beyond the Early Adopters, because the companies that make them can't find a way to transform an idea that makes perfect sense to an Early Adopter into one that makes perfect sense to a member of the Early Majority.

Moore's book is entirely concerned with high technology. But there's no question that his arguments apply to other kinds of social epidemics as well. In the case of Hush Puppies, the downtown Manhattan kids who rediscovered the brand were wearing the shoes because Hush Puppies were identified with a dated, kitschy, fifties image. They were wearing them precisely because no one else would wear them. What they were looking for in fashion was a revolutionary statement. They were willing to take risks in order to set themselves apart. But most of us in the Early and Late Majority don't want to make a revolutionary statement or take risks with fashion at all. How did Hush Puppies cross the chasm from one group to the next? Lambesis was given a shoe that had a very specific appeal to the southern California skateboarding subculture. Their task was to make it hip and attractive to teenagers all over the world — even teens who had never skateboarded in their life, who didn't think skateboarding was particularly cool, and who had no functional need for wide outsoles that could easily grip the board and padded uppers to cushion the shocks of doing aerial stunts. That's clearly not an easy task either. How did they do it? How is it that all the weird, idiosyncratic things that really cool kids do end up in the mainstream?

This is where, I think, Connectors, Mavens, and Salesmen play their most important role. In the chapter on the Law of the Few, I talked about how their special social gifts can cause epidemics to tip. Here, though, it is possible to be much more specific about what they do. They are the ones who make it possible for innovations to overcome this problem of the chasm. They are translators: they take ideas and information from a highly specialized world and translate them into a language the rest of us can understand. Mark Alpert, the University of Texas professor whom I described as the Ur-Maven, is the kind of person who would come over to your house and show you how to install or fix or manipulate a very complicated piece of software. Tom Gau, the quintessential Salesman, takes the very arcane field of tax law and retirement planning and repackages it in terms that make emotional sense to his clients. Lois Weisberg, the Connector, belongs to many different worlds — politics, drama, environmentalism, music, law, medicine, and on and on — and one of the key things she does is to play the intermediary between different social worlds. One of the key figures at Lambesis was DeeDee Gordon, the firm's former head of market research, and she says that the same process occurs in the case of the fashion trends that periodically sweep through youth culture. The Innovators try something new. Then someone — the teen equivalent of a Maven or a Connector or a Salesman — sees it and adopts it. "Those kids make things more palatable for mainstream people. They see what the really wired kids are doing and they tweak it. They start doing it themselves, but they change it a bit. They make it more usable. Maybe there's a kid who rolls up his jeans and puts duct tape around the bottom because he's the one bike messenger in the school. Well, the translators like that look. But they won't use tape. They'll buy something with Velcro. Or then there was the whole baby-doll T-shirt thing. One girl starts wearing a shrunken-down T-shirt.

She goes to Toys R Us and buys the Barbie T-shirt. And the others say, that's so cool. But they might not get it so small, and they might not get it with Barbie on it. They look at it and say, it's a little off. But there's a way I can change it and make it okay. Then it takes off."

Perhaps the most sophisticated analysis of this process of translation comes from the study of rumors, which are — obviously — the most contagious of all social messages. In his book *The Psychology of Rumor,* the sociologist Gordon Allport writes of a rumor involving a Chinese teacher who was traveling through Maine on vacation in the summer of 1945, shortly before Japan's surrender to the Allies at the end of World War II. The teacher was carrying a guidebook, which said that a splendid view of the surrounding countryside could be seen from a certain local hilltop, and he stopped in a small town to ask directions. From that innocent request, a rumor quickly spread: a Japanese spy had gone up the hill to take pictures of the region. "The simple, unadorned facts that constitute the 'kernel of truth' in this rumor," Allport writes, "were from the outset distorted in . . . three directions." First of all the story was *leveled.* All kinds of details that are essential for understanding the true meaning of the incident were left out. There was no mention, Allport points out, of "the courteous and timid approach of the visitor to the native of whom he inquired his way; the fact that the visitor's precise nationality was unknown, . . . the fact that the visitor had allowed himself to be readily identified by people along the way." Then the story was *sharpened.* The details that remained were made more specific. A man became a spy. Someone who looked

Asian became Japanese. Sightseeing became espionage. The guidebook in the teacher's hand became a camera. Finally, a process of *assimilation* took place: the story was changed so it made more sense to those spreading the rumor. "A Chinese teacher on a holiday was a concept that could not arise in the minds of most farmers, for they did not know that some American universities employ Chinese scholars on their staffs and that these scholars, like other teachers, are entitled to summer holidays," Allport writes. "The novel situation was perforce assimilated in terms of the most available frames of reference." And what were those frames of reference? In 1945, in rural Maine, at a time when virtually every family had a son or relative involved in the war effort, the only way to make sense of a story like that was to fit it into the context of the war. Thus did Asian become Japanese, guidebook become camera, and sightseeing become espionage.

Psychologists have found that this process of distortion is nearly universal in the spread of rumors. Memory experiments have been done in which subjects are given a story to read or a picture to look at and then asked to return, at intervals of several months, and reproduce what they had been shown. Invariably, significant leveling occurs. All but a few details are dropped. But certain details are also, simultaneously, sharpened. In one classic example, subjects were given a drawing of a hexagon bisected by three lines with seven equal-size circles superimposed on top of it. What one typical subject remembered, several months later, was a square bisected by two lines with 38 small circles arrayed around the fringes of the diagram. "There was a marked tendency for any picture or story to gravitate in memory toward what was familiar to the subject in his own life, consonant with his own culture, and above all, to what had some special emotional significance for him," Allport writes. "In their effort after meaning, the subjects would condense or fill in so as to achieve a better 'Gestalt,' a better closure — a simpler, more significant configuration."

This is what is meant by translation. What Mavens and Connectors and Salesmen do to an idea in order to make it contagious is to alter it in such a way that extraneous details are dropped and others are exaggerated so that the message itself comes to acquire a deeper meaning. If anyone wants to start an epidemic, then — whether it is of shoes or behavior or a piece of software — he or she has to somehow employ Connectors, Mavens, and Salesmen in this very way: he or she has to find some person or some means to translate the message of the Innovators into something the rest of us can understand.

2.

There is a wonderful example of this strategy in action in Baltimore, the city whose problems with drugs and disease I talked about earlier in the book. In Baltimore, as in many communities with a lot of drug addicts, the city sends out a van stocked with thousands of clean syringes to certain street corners in its inner-city neighborhoods at certain times in the week. The idea is that for every dirty, used needle that addicts hand over, they can get a free clean needle in return. In principle, needle exchange sounds like a good way to fight AIDS, since the reuse of old

HIV-infected needles is responsible for so much of the virus's spread. But, at least on first examination, it seems to have some obvious limitations. Addicts, for one, aren't the most organized and reliable of people. So what guarantee is there that they are going to be able to regularly meet up with the needle van? Second, most heroin addicts go through about one needle a day, shooting up at least five or six times — if not more — until the tip of the syringe becomes so blunt that it is useless. That's a lot of needles. How can a van, coming by once a week, serve the needs of addicts who are shooting up around the clock? What if the van comes by on Tuesday, and by Saturday night an addict has run out?

To analyze how well the needle program was working, researchers at Johns Hopkins University began, in the mid-1990s, to ride along with the vans in order to talk to the people handing in needles. What they found surprised them. They had assumed that addicts brought in their own dirty needles for exchange, that IV drug users got new needles the way that you or I buy milk: going to the store when it is open and picking up enough for the week. But what they found was that a handful of addicts were coming by each week with knapsacks bulging with 300 or 400 dirty needles at a time, which is obviously far more than they were using themselves. These men were then going back to the street and selling the clean needles for one dollar each. The van, in other words, was a kind of syringe wholesaler. The real retailers were these handfuls of men — these super-exchangers — who were prowling around the streets and shooting galleries, picking up dirty needles, and then making a modest living on the clean needles they received in exchange. At first, some of the program's coordinators had second thoughts. Did they really want taxpayer-funded needles financing the habits of addicts? But then they realized that they had stumbled inadvertently into a solution to the limitations of needle exchange programs. "It's a much, much better system," says Tom Valente, who teaches in the Johns Hopkins School of Public Health. "A lot of people shoot on Friday and Saturday night, and they don't necessarily think in a rational way that they need to have clean tools before they go out. The needle exchange program isn't going to be available at that time — and certainly not in the shooting galleries. But these [super-exchangers] can be there at times when people are doing drugs and when they need clean syringes. They provide twenty-four seven service, and it doesn't cost us anything."

One of the researchers who rode with the needle vans was an epidemiologist by the name of Tom Junge. He would flag down the super-exchangers and interview them. His conclusion is that they represent a very distinct and special group. "They are all very well connected people," Junge says. "They know Baltimore inside and out. They know where to go to get any kind of drug and any kind of needle. They have street savvy. I would say that they are unusually socially connected. They have a lot of contacts. . . . I would have to say the underlying motive is financial or economic. But there is definitely an interest in helping people out."

Does this sound familiar? The super-exchangers are the Connectors of Baltimore's drug world. What people at Johns Hopkins would like to do is use the

super-exchangers to start a counter–drug epidemic. What
if they took those same savvy, socially connected, altruistic
people and gave them condoms to hand out, or educated
them in the kinds of health information that drug addicts
desperately need to know? Those super-exchangers sound
as though they have the skills to bridge the chasm between
the medical community and the majority of drug users,
who are hopelessly isolated from the information and
institutions that could save their lives. They sound as if
they have the ability to translate the language and ideas of
health promotion into a form that other addicts could
understand.

3.

Lambesis's intention was to perform this very same service
for Airwalk. Obviously, they couldn't directly identify the
equivalent of Mavens and Connectors and Salesmen to
spread the word about Airwalk. They were a tiny ad
agency trying to put together an international campaign.
What they could do, though, was start an epidemic in
which their own ad campaign played the role of translator,
serving as an intermediary between the Innovators and
everyone else. If they did their homework right, they realized, they could be the ones to level and sharpen and
assimilate the cutting-edge ideas of youth culture and
make them acceptable for the Majority. They could play
the role of Connector, Maven, and Salesman.

The first thing Lambesis did was to develop an in-
house market research program, aimed at the youth market
that Airwalk wanted to conquer. If they were going to

translate Innovator ideas for the mainstream, they first had to find out what those Innovator ideas were. To run their research division, Lambesis hired DeeDee Gordon, who had previously worked for the Converse athletic shoe company. Gordon is a striking woman, with a languid wit, who lives in a right-angled, shag-rugged, white-stuccoed modernist masterpiece in the Hollywood Hills, midway between Madonna's old house and Aldous Huxley's old house. Her tastes are almost impossibly eclectic: depending on the day of the week, she might be obsessed with an obscure hip-hop band, or an old Peter Sellers movie, or a new Japanese electronic gadget, or a certain shade of white that she has suddenly, mysteriously, decided is very cool. While she was at Converse Gordon noticed white teenage girls in Los Angeles dressing up like Mexican gangsters with the look they called "the wife beater" — a tight white tank top with the bra straps showing — and long shorts and tube socks and shower sandals. "I told them, this is going to hit," Gordon remembers. "There are just too many people wearing it. We have to make a shower sandal." So they cut the back off a Converse sneaker, put a sandal outsole on it, and Converse sold half a million pairs. Gordon has a sixth sense of what neighborhoods or bars or clubs to go to in London or Tokyo or Berlin to find out what the latest looks and fashion are. She sometimes comes to New York and sits watching the sidewalks of Soho and the East Village for hours, photographing anything unusual. Gordon is a Maven — a Maven for the elusive, indefinable quality known as cool.

At Lambesis, Gordon developed a network of young, savvy correspondents in New York and Los Angeles and

Chicago and Dallas and Seattle and around the world in places like Tokyo and London. These were the kind of people who would have been wearing Hush Puppies in the East Village in the early 1990s. They all fit a particular personality type: they were Innovators.

"These are kids who are outcasts in some way," Gordon says. "It doesn't matter whether it's actually true. They feel that way. They always felt like they were different. If you ask kids what worries them, the trendsetter kids pick up on things like germ warfare, or terrorism. They pick up on bigger-picture things, whereas the mainstream kids think about being overweight, or their grandparents dying, or how well they are doing in school. You see more activists in trendsetters. People with more passion. I'm looking for somebody who is an individual, who has definitely set herself apart from everybody else, who doesn't look like their peers."

Gordon has a kind of relentless curiosity about the world. "I've run into trendsetters who look completely Joe Regular Guy," she went on. "I can see Joe Regular Guy at a club listening to some totally hard-core band playing, and I say to myself, omigod, what's that guy doing here, and that totally intrigues me, and I have to walk up to him and say, hey, you're really into this band. What's up? You know what I mean? I look at everything. If I see Joe Regular Guy sitting in a coffee shop and everyone around him has blue hair, I'm going to gravitate toward him because, hey, what's Joe Regular Guy doing in a coffee shop with people with blue hair?"

With her stable of Innovator correspondents in place, Gordon would then go back to them two or three or four times a year, asking them what music they were listening to, what television shows they were watching, what clothes they were buying, or what their goals and aspirations were. The data were not always coherent. They required interpretation. Different ideas would pop up in different parts of the country, then sometimes move east to west or sometimes west to east. But by looking at the big picture, by comparing the data from Austin to Seattle and Seattle to Los Angeles and Los Angeles to New York, and watching it change from one month to the next, Gordon was able to develop a picture of the rise and movement of new trends across the country. And by comparing what her Innovators were saying and doing with what mainstream kids were saying and doing three months or six months or a year later, she was able to track what sorts of ideas were able to make the jump from the cool subcultures to the Majority.

"Take the whole men-wearing-makeup, the Kurt Cobain, androgynous thing," Gordon said. "You know how he used to paint his fingernails with Magic Marker? We saw that in the Northwest first, then trickling through Los Angeles and New York and Austin because they have a hip music scene. Then it trickled into other parts of the country. That took a long time to go mainstream."

Gordon's findings became the template for the Airwalk campaign. If she found new trends or ideas or concepts that were catching fire among Innovators around the country, the firm would plant those same concepts in the Airwalk ads they were creating. Once, for example, Gordon picked up on the fact that trendsetters were developing a sudden interest in Tibet and the Dalai Lama. The influential rap band Beastie Boys were very publicly putting money into the Free Tibet campaign, and were bringing monks on stage at their concerts to give testimonials. "The Beastie Boys pushed that through and made it okay," Gordon remembers. So Lambesis made a very funny Airwalk ad with a young Airwalk-wearing monk sitting at a desk in a classroom writing a test. He's looking down at his feet because he's written cheat notes on the side of his shoes. (When a billboard version of the ad was put up in San Francisco, Lambesis was forced to take it down, after Tibetan monks protested that monks don't touch their feet, let alone cheat on tests.) When James Bond started popping up on the trendsetter radar, Lambesis hired the director of the James Bond movies to film a series of commercials, all of which featured Airwalk-clad characters making wild escapes from faceless villains. When trendsetters started to show an ironic interest in country club culture, and began wearing old Fred Perry and Izod golf shirts, Airwalk made a shoe out of tennis ball material and Lambesis made a print ad of the shoe being thrown up in the air and hit with a tennis racket. "One time we noticed that the future technology thing was really big," Gordon says. "You'd ask some kid what they would invent, if they could invent anything they wanted, and it was always about effortless living. You know, put your head in a bubble, push a button, and it comes out perfect. So we got Airwalk to do these rounded, bubbly outsoles for the shoes. We started mixing materials — meshes and breathable materials and special types of Gore-Tex and laying them on top of each other." To look through the inventory of Airwalk ads in that critical period, in fact, is to get a complete guide to the fads and infatuations and interests of the youth culture of the era: there are 30-second spoofs of kung fu movies, a TV spot on Beat poetry, an *X-files*–style commercial in which a young man driving into Roswell, New Mexico, has his Airwalks confiscated by aliens.

There are two explanations for why this strategy was so successful. The first is obvious. Lambesis was picking on various, very contagious, trends while they were still in their infancy. By the time their new ad campaign and the shoes to go along with it were ready, that trend (with luck) would just be hitting the mainstream. Lambesis, in other words, was piggy-backing on social epidemics, associating Airwalk with each new trend wave that swept through youth culture. "It's all about timing," Gordon says. "You follow the trendsetters. You see what they are doing. It takes a year to produce those shoes. By the time the year goes, if your trend is the right trend, it's going to hit those mainstream people at the right time. So if you see future technology as a trend — if you see enough trendsetters in enough cities buying things that are ergonomic in design, or shoes that are jacked up, or little Palm Pilots, and when you ask them to invent something, they're all talking about flying cars of the future — that's going to lead you to believe that within six months to a year everyone and his grandmother will be into the same thing."

Lambesis wasn't just a passive observer in this process, however. It is also the case that their ads helped to tip the ideas they were discovering among Innovators. Gordon says, for example, that when something fails to make it out of the trendsetter community into the mainstream, it's usually because the idea doesn't root itself broadly enough in the culture: "There aren't enough cues. You didn't see it in music and film and art and fashion. Usually, if something's going to make it, you'll see that thread running throughout everything — through what they like on TV, what they want to invent, what they want to listen to, even the materials they want to wear. It's everywhere. But if something doesn't make it, you'll only see it in one of those areas." Lambesis was taking certain ideas, and planting them everywhere. And as they planted them, they provided that critical translation. Gordon's research showed that Innovator kids were heavily into the Dalai Lama and all of the very serious issues raised by the occupation of Tibet. So Lambesis took one very simple reference to that — a Tibetan monk — and put him in a funny, slightly cheeky situation. They tweaked it. The Innovators had a heavily ironic interest in country club culture. Lambesis lightened that. They made the shoe into a tennis ball, and that made the reference less arch and more funny. Innovators were into kung fu movies. So Lambesis made a kung fu parody ad in which the Airwalk hero fights off martial arts villains with his skateboard. Lambesis took the kung fu motif and merged it with youth culture. In the case of the Chinese scholar's vacation, according to Allport, the facts of the situation didn't make sense to the people of the town; so they came up with an interpretation that did make sense — that the scholar was a spy — and, to make that new interpretation work, "discordant details were leveled out, incidents were sharpened to fit the chosen theme, and the episode as a whole was assimilated to the preexisting structure of feeling and thought characteristic of the members of the group among whom the rumor spread." That's just what Lambesis did. They took the cultural cues from the Innovators — cues that the mainstream kids may have seen but not been able to make sense of — and leveled, sharpened, and assimilated them into a more coherent form. They gave those cues a specific meaning that they did not have previously and packaged that new sensibility in the form of a pair of shoes. It can hardly be a surprise that the Airwalk rumor spread so quickly in 1995 and 1996.

4.

The Airwalk epidemic did not last. In 1997, the company's sales began to falter. The firm had production problems and difficulty filling their orders. In critical locations, Airwalk failed to supply enough product for the back-to-school season, and its once loyal distributors began to turn against it. At the same time, the company began to lose that cutting-edge sensibility that it had traded on for so long. "When Airwalk started, the product was directional and inventive. The shoes were very forward," said Chad Farmer. "We maintained the trendsetter focus on the marketing. But the product began to slip. The company began to listen more and more to the sales staff and the product started to get that homogenized, mainstream look. Everybody loved the marketing. In focus groups that we do, they still talk about how they miss it. But the number one complaint is, what happened to the cool product?" Lambesis's strategy was based on translating Innovator shoes for the Majority. But suddenly Airwalk wasn't an Innovator shoe anymore. "We made another, critical mistake," Lee Smith, the former president of Airwalk says. "We had a segmentation strategy, where the small, independent core skate shops — the three hundred boutiques around the country who really created us — had a certain product line that was exclusive to them. They didn't want us to be in the mall. So what we did was, we segmented our product. We said to the core shops, you don't have to compete with the malls. It worked out very well." The boutiques were given the technical shoes: different designs, better materials, more padding, different cushioning systems, different rubber compounds, more expensive uppers. "We had a special signature model — the Tony Hawk — for skateboarding, which was a lot beefier and more durable. It would retail for about eighty dollars." The shoes Airwalk distributed to Kinney's or Champ's or Foot Locker, meanwhile, were less elaborate and would retail for about $60. The Innovators always got to wear a different, more exclusive shoe than everyone else. The mainstream customer had the satisfaction of wearing the same brand as the cool kids.

But then, at the height of its success, Airwalk switched strategies. The company stopped giving the specialty shops their own shoes. "That's when the trendsetters started to get a disregard for the brand," says Farmer. "They started to go to their boutiques where they got their cool stuff, and they realized that everyone else could get the very same shoes at J C Penney." Now, all of a sudden, Lambesis was translating the language of mainstream products for the mainstream. The epidemic was over.

"My category manager once asked me what happened," Smith says, "and I told him, you ever see *Forrest*

Gump? Stupid is as stupid does. Well, cool is as cool does. Cool brands treat people well, and we didn't. I had personally promised some of those little shops that we would give them special product, then we changed our minds. That was the beginning. In that world, it all works on word of mouth. When we became bigger, that's when we should have paid more attention to the details and kept a good buzz going, so when people said you guys are sellouts, you guys went mainstream, you suck, we could have said, you know what, we don't. We had this little jewel of a brand, and little by little we sold that off into the mainstream, and once we had sold it all" — he paused — "so what? You buy a pair of our shoes. Why would you ever buy another?"

SEVEN

Case Study

SUICIDE, SMOKING, AND THE SEARCH FOR THE UNSTICKY CIGARETTE

N ot long ago, on the South Pacific islands of Micronesia, a seventeen-year-old boy named Sima got into an argument with his father. He was staying with his family at his grandfather's house when his father — a stern and demanding man — ordered him out of bed early one morning and told him to find a bamboo pole-knife to harvest breadfruit. Sima spent hours in the village, looking without success for a pole-knife, and when he returned empty-handed, his father was furious. The family would now go hungry, he told his son, waving a machete in rage. "Get out of here and go find somewhere else to live."

Sima left his grandfather's house and walked back to his home village. Along the way he ran into his fourteen-year-old brother and borrowed a pen. Two hours later, curious about where Sima had gone, his brother went looking for him. He returned to the now empty family house and peered in the window. In the middle of a dark room, hanging slack and still from a noose, was Sima. He was dead. His suicide note read:

> My life is coming to an end at this time. Now today is a day of sorrow for myself, also a day of suffering for me. But it is a day of celebration for Papa. Today Papa sent me away. Thank you for loving me so little. Sima.
>
> Give my farewell to Mama. Mama you won't have any more frustration or trouble from your boy. Much love from Sima.

In the early 1960s, suicide on the islands of Micronesia was almost unknown. But for reasons no one quite understands, it then began to rise, steeply and dramatically, by leaps and bounds every year, until by the end of the 1980s there were more suicides per capita in Micronesia than anywhere else in the world. For males between fifteen and twenty-four, the suicide rate in the United States is about 22 per 100,000. In the islands of Micronesia the rate is about 160 per 100,000 — more than seven times higher. At that level, suicide is almost commonplace, triggered by the smallest of incidents. Sima took his own life because his father yelled at him. In the midst of the Micronesian epidemic, that was hardly unusual. Teens committed suicide on the islands because they saw their girlfriends with another boy, or because their parents refused to give them a few extra dollars for beer. One nineteen-year-old hanged himself because his parents didn't buy him a graduation gown. One seventeen-year-old hanged himself because he had been rebuked by his older brother for making too much noise. What, in Western cultures, is something rare, random, and deeply pathological, has become in Micronesia a ritual of adolescence, with its own particular rules and symbols. Virtually all suicides on the islands, in fact, are identical variations on Sima's story. The victim is almost always male. He is in his late teens, unmarried, and living at home. The precipitating event is invariably domestic: a dispute with girlfriends or parents. In three-quarters of the cases, the victim had never tried — or even threatened — suicide before. The suicide notes tend to express not depression but a kind of wounded pride and self-pity, a protest against mistreatment. The act itself typically occurs on a weekend night, usually after a bout of drinking with friends. In all but a few cases, the victim observes the same procedure, as if there were a strict, unwritten protocol about the correct way to take one's own life. He finds a remote spot or empty house. He takes a rope and makes a noose, but he does not suspend himself, as in a typical Western hanging. He ties the noose to a low branch or a window or a doorknob and leans forward, so that the weight of his body draws the noose tightly around his neck, cutting off the flow of blood to the brain. Unconsciousness follows. Death results from anoxia — the shortage of blood to the brain.

In Micronesia, the anthropologist Donald Rubinstein writes, these rituals have become embedded in the local culture. As the number of suicides have grown, the idea has fed upon itself, infecting younger and younger boys, and transforming the act itself so that the unthinkable has somehow been rendered thinkable. According to Rubinstein, who has documented the Micronesian epidemic in a series of brilliant papers,

> Suicide ideation among adolescents appears widespread in certain Micronesian communities and is popularly expressed in recent songs composed locally and aired on Micronesian radio stations, and in graffiti adorning T-shirts and high school walls. A number of young boys who attempted suicide reported that they first saw or heard about it when they were 8 or 10 years old. Their suicide attempts appear in the spirit of imitative or experimental play. One 11-year-old boy, for example, hanged himself inside his house and when found he was already unconscious and his tongue protruding. He later explained that he wanted to "try" out hanging. He said that he did not want to die, although he knew he was risking death. Such cases of imitative suicide attempts by boys as young as five and six have been reported recently from Truk. Several cases of young adolescent suicide deaths recently in Micronesia were evidently the outcome of such experiments. Thus as suicide grows more frequent in these communities the idea itself acquires a certain familiarity if not fascination to young men, and the lethality of the act seems to be trivialized. Especially among some younger boys, the suicide acts appear to have acquired an experimental almost recreational element.

There is something very chilling about this passage. Suicide isn't supposed to be trivialized like this. But the truly chilling thing about it is how familiar it all seems. Here we have a contagious epidemic of self-destruction, engaged in by youth in the spirit of experimentation, imitation, and rebellion. Here we have a mindless action that somehow, among teenagers, has become an important form of self-expression. In a strange way, the Micronesian teen suicide epidemic sounds an awful lot like the epidemic of teenage smoking in the West.

1.

Teenage smoking is one of the great, baffling phenomena of modern life. No one really knows how to fight it, or even, for that matter, what it is. The principal assumption of the anti-smoking movement has been that tobacco companies persuade teens to smoke by lying to them, by making smoking sound a lot more desirable and a lot less harmful than it really is. To address that problem, then, we've restricted and policed cigarette advertising, so it's a lot harder for tobacco companies to lie. We've raised the price of cigarettes and enforced the law against selling tobacco to minors, to try to make it much harder for teens to buy cigarettes. And we've run extensive public health campaigns on television and radio and in magazines to try to educate teens about the dangers of smoking.

It has become fairly obvious, however, that this approach isn't very effective. Why do we think, for example, that the key to fighting smoking is educating people about the risks of cigarettes? Harvard University economist W. Kip Viscusi recently asked a group of smokers to guess how many years of life, on average, smoking from the age of twenty-one onward would cost them. They guessed nine years. The real answer is somewhere around six or

seven. Smokers aren't smokers because they under-
estimate the risks of smoking. They smoke even though
they overestimate the risk of smoking. At the same time, it
is not clear how effective it is to have adults tell teenagers
that they shouldn't smoke. As any parent of a teenage
child will tell you, the essential contrariness of adolescents
suggests that the more adults inveigh against smoking and
lecture teenagers about its dangers, the more teens, para-
doxically, will want to try it. Sure enough, if you look at
smoking trends over the past decade or so, that is exactly
what has happened. The anti-smoking movement has
never been louder or more prominent. Yet all signs suggest
that among the young the anti-smoking message is back-
firing. Between 1993 and 1997, the number of college students who smoke jumped from 22.3 percent to 28.5
percent. Between 1991 and 1997, the number of high
school students who smoke jumped 32 percent. Since
1988, in fact, the total number of teen smokers in the
United States has risen an extraordinary 73 percent. There
are few public health programs in recent years that have
fallen as short of their mission as the war on smoking.

The lesson here is not that we should give up trying to
fight cigarettes. The point is simply that the way we have
tended to think about the causes of smoking doesn't make
a lot of sense. That's why the epidemic of suicide in
Micronesia is so interesting and potentially relevant to the
smoking problem. It gives us another way of trying to
come to terms with youth smoking. What if smoking,
instead of following the rational principles of the marketplace, follows the same kind of mysterious and complex

social rules and rituals that govern teen suicide? If smoking really is an epidemic like Micronesian suicide, how does that change the way we ought to fight the problem?

2.

The central observation of those who study suicide is that, in some places and under some circumstances, the act of one person taking his or her own life can be contagious. Suicides lead to suicides. The pioneer in this field is David Phillips, a sociologist at the University of California at San Diego, who has conducted a number of studies on suicide, each more fascinating and seemingly improbable than the last. He began by making a list of all the stories about suicide that ran on the front page of the country's most prominent newspapers in the twenty-year stretch between the end of the 1940s and the end of the 1960s. Then he matched them up with suicide statistics from the same period. He wanted to know whether there was any relationship between the two. Sure enough, there was. Immediately after stories about suicides appeared, suicides in the area served by the newspaper jumped. In the case of national stories, the rate jumped nationally. (Marilyn Monroe's death was followed by a temporary 12 percent increase in the national suicide rate.) Then Phillips repeated his experiment with traffic accidents. He took front-page suicide stories from the *Los Angeles Times* and the *San Francisco Chronicle* and matched them up with traffic fatalities from the state of California. He found the same pattern. On the day after a highly publicized suicide, the number of fatalities from traffic accidents was, on average,

5.9 percent higher than expected. Two days after a suicide story, traffic deaths rose 4.1 percent. Three days after, they rose 3.1 percent, and four days after, they rose 8.1 percent. (After ten days, the traffic fatality rate was back to normal.) Phillips concluded that one of the ways in which people commit suicide is by deliberately crashing their cars, and that these people were just as susceptible to the contagious effects of a highly publicized suicide as were people killing themselves by more conventional means.

The kind of contagion Phillips is talking about isn't something rational or even necessarily conscious. It's not like a persuasive argument. It's something much more subtle than that. "When I'm waiting at a traffic light and the light is red, sometimes I wonder whether I should cross and jaywalk," he says. "Then somebody else does it and so I do too. It's a kind of imitation. I'm getting permission to act from someone else who is engaging in a deviant act. Is that a conscious decision? I can't tell. Maybe afterwards I could brood on the difference. But at the time I don't know whether any of us knows how much of our decision is conscious and how much is unconscious. Human decisions are subtle and complicated and not very well understood." In the case of suicide, Phillips argues, the decision by someone famous to take his or her own life has the same effect: it gives other people, particularly those vulnerable to suggestion because of immaturity or mental illness, permission to engage in a deviant act as well. "Suicide stories are a kind of natural advertisement for a particular response to your problems," Phillips continues. "You've got all these people who are unhappy and have difficulty making up their minds because they are

depressed. They are living with this pain. There are lots of
stories advertising different kinds of responses to that. It
could be that Billy Graham has a crusade going on that
weekend — that's a religious response. Or it could be that
somebody is advertising an escapist movie — that's
another response. Suicide stories offer another kind of
alternative." Phillips's permission-givers are the functional
equivalent of the Salesmen I talked about in chapter 2. Just
as Tom Gau could, through the persuasive force of his personality, serve as a Tipping Point in a word-of-mouth epidemic, the people who die in highly publicized suicides —
whose deaths give others "permission" to die — serve as
the Tipping Points in suicide epidemics.

The fascinating thing about this permission-giving,
though, is how extraordinarily specific it is. In his study of
motor fatalities, Phillips found a clear pattern. Stories
about suicides resulted in an increase in single-car crashes
where the victim was the driver. Stories about suicide-
murders resulted in an increase in multiple-car crashes in
which the victims included both drivers and passengers.
Stories about young people committing suicide resulted in
more traffic fatalities involving young people. Stories
about older people committing suicide resulted in more
traffic fatalities involving older people. These patterns have
been demonstrated on many occasions. News coverage of
a number of suicides by self-immolation in England in the
late 1970s, for example, prompted 82 suicides by self-
immolation over the next year. The "permission" given by
an initial act of suicide, in other words, isn't a general invitation to the vulnerable. It is really a highly detailed set of
instructions, specific to certain people in certain situations

who choose to die in certain ways. It's not a gesture. It's speech. In another study, a group of researchers in England in the 1960s analyzed 135 people who had been admitted to a central psychiatric hospital after attempting suicide. They found that the group was strongly linked socially — that many of them belonged to the same social circles. This, they concluded, was not coincidence. It testified to the very essence of what suicide is, a private language between members of a common subculture. The author's conclusion is worth quoting in full:

> Many patients who attempt suicide are drawn from a section of the community in which self-aggression is generally recognized as a means of conveying a certain kind of information. Among this group the act is viewed as comprehensible and consistent with the rest of the cultural pattern. . . . If this is true, it follows that the individual who in particular situations, usually of distress, wishes to convey information about his difficulties to others, does not have to invent a communicational medium de novo. . . . The individual within the "attempted suicide subculture" can perform an act which carries a preformed meaning; all he is required to do is invoke it. The process is essentially similar to that whereby a person uses a word in a spoken language.

This is what is going on in Micronesia, only at a much more profound level. If suicide in the West is a kind of crude language, in Micronesia it has become an incredibly expressive form of communication, rich with meaning and nuance, and expressed by the most persuasive of permission-givers. Rubinstein writes of the strange pattern of suicides on the Micronesian island of Ebeye, a community of about 6,000. Between 1955 and 1965, there wasn't a single case of suicide on the entire island. In May 1966, an eighteen-year-old boy hanged himself in his jail cell after being arrested for stealing a bicycle, but his case seemed to have little impact. Then, in November of 1966, came the death of R., the charismatic scion of one of the island's wealthiest families. R. had been seeing two women and had fathered a one-month-old child with each of them. Unable to make up his mind between them, he hanged himself in romantic despair. At his funeral, his two lovers, learning of the existence of the other for the first time, fainted on his grave.

Three days after R.'s death, there was another suicide, a twenty-two-year-old male suffering from marital difficulties, bringing the suicide toll to two over a week in a community that had seen one suicide in the previous twelve years. The island's medic wrote: "After R. died, many boys dreamed about him and said that he was calling them to kill themselves." Twenty-five more suicides followed over the next twelve years, mostly in clusters of three or four over the course of a few weeks. "Several suicide victims and several who have recently attempted suicide reported having a vision in which a boat containing all the past victims circles the island with the deceased inviting the potential victims to join them," a visiting anthropologist wrote in 1975. Over and over again, the themes outlined by R. resurfaced. Here is the suicide note of M., a high school student who had one girlfriend at boarding school and one girlfriend on Ebeye, and when the first girlfriend returned home from school, two girlfriends at once — a complication defined, in the youth sub-culture of Ebeye, as grounds for taking one's own life: "Best wishes to M. and C. [the two girlfriends]. It's been nice to be with both of you." That's all he had to say, because the context for his act had already been created by R. In the Ebeye epidemic, R. was the Tipping Person, the Salesman, the one whose experience "overwrote" the experience of those who followed him. The power of his personality and the circumstances of his death combined to make the force of his example endure years beyond his death.

3.

Does teen smoking follow this same logic? In order to find out more about the reasons teenagers smoke, I gave several hundred people a questionnaire, asking them to describe their earliest experiences with cigarettes. This was not a scientific study. The sample wasn't representative of the United States. It was mostly people in their late twenties and early thirties, living in big cities. Nonetheless the answers were striking, principally because of how similar they all seemed. Smoking seemed to evoke a particular kind of childhood memory — vivid, precise, emotionally charged. One person remembers how she loved to open her grandmother's purse, where she would encounter "the soft smell of cheap Winstons and leather mixed with drug store lipstick and cinnamon gum." Another remembers "sitting in the back seat of a Chrysler sedan, smelling the wonderful mixture of sulfur and tobacco waft out the driver's window and into my nostrils." Smoking, overwhelmingly, was associated with the same thing to nearly everyone: sophistication. This was true even of people who now hate smoking, who now think of it as a dirty and dangerous habit. The language of smoking, like the language of suicide, seems incredibly consistent. Here are two responses, both describing childhood memories:

> My mother smoked, and even though I hated it — hated the smell — she had these long tapered fingers and full, sort of crinkly lips, always with lipstick on, and when she smoked she looked so elegant and devil-may-care that there was no question that I'd smoke someday. She thought people who didn't smoke were kind of gutless. Makes you stink, makes you think, she would say, reveling in how ugly that sounded.

> My best friend Susan was Irish-English. Her parents were, in contrast to mine, youthful, indulgent, liberal. They had cocktails before dinner. Mr. O'Sullivan had a beard and wore turtlenecks. Mrs. O'Sullivan tottered around in mules, dressed slimly in black to match her jet-black hair. She wore heavy eye-makeup and was a little too tan and always, virtually always, had a dangerously long cigarette holder dangling from her manicured hands.

This is the shared language of smoking, and it is as rich and expressive as the shared language of suicide. In this epidemic, as well, there are also Tipping People, Salesmen, permission-givers. Time and time again, the respondents to my survey described the particular individual who initiated them into smoking in precisely the same way.

When I was around nine or ten my parents got an English au pair girl, Maggie, who came and stayed with us one summer. She was maybe twenty. She was very sexy and wore a bikini at the Campbells' pool. She was famous with the grownup men for doing handstands in her bikini. Also it was said her bikini top fell off when she dove — Mr. Carpenter would submerge whenever she jumped in. Maggie smoked, and I used to beg her to let me smoke too.

The first kid I knew who smoked was Billy G. We became friends in fifth grade, when the major distinctions in our suburban N.J. town — jocks, heads, brains — were beginning to form. Billy was incredibly cool. He was the first kid to date girls, smoke cigarettes and pot, drink hard alcohol and listen to druggy music. I even remember sitting upstairs in his sister's bedroom — his parents were divorced (another first), and his mom was never home — separating the seeds out of some pot on the cover of a Grateful Dead album. . . . The draw for me was the badness of it, and the adult-ness, and the way it proved the idea that you could be more than one thing at once.

The first person who I remember smoking was a girl named Pam P. I met her when we were both in the 10th grade. We rode the school bus together in Great Neck, L.I., and I remember thinking she was the coolest because she lived in an apartment. (Great Neck didn't have many apartments.) Pam seemed so much older than her 15 years. We used to sit in the back of the bus and blow smoke out the window. She taught me how to inhale, how to tie a man-tailored shirt at the waist to look cool, and how to wear lipstick. She had a leather jacket. Her father was rarely home.

There is actually considerable support for this idea that there is a common personality to hard-core smokers. Hans Eysenck, the influential British psychologist, has argued that serious smokers can be separated from non-smokers along very simple personality lines. The quintessential hard-core smoker, according to Eysenck, is an extrovert, the kind of person who

> is sociable, likes parties, has many friends, needs to have people to talk to.... He craves excitement, takes chances, acts on the spur of the moment and is generally an impulsive individual.... He prefers to keep moving and doing things, tends to be aggressive and loses his temper quickly; his feelings are not kept under tight control and he is not always a reliable person.

In countless studies since Eysenck's groundbreaking work, this picture of the smoking "type" has been filled out. Heavy smokers have been shown to have a much greater sex drive than nonsmokers. They are more sexually precocious; they have a greater "need" for sex, and greater attraction to the opposite sex. At age nineteen, for example, 15 percent of nonsmoking white women attending college have had sex. The same number for white female college students who do smoke is 55 percent. The statistics for men are about the same according to Eysenck. They rank much higher on what psychologists call "anti-social" indexes: they tend to have greater levels of misconduct, and be more rebellious and defiant. They make snap judgments. They take more risks. The average smoking household spends 73 percent more on coffee and two to three times as much on beer as the average non-smoking household. Interestingly, smokers also seem to be more honest about themselves than nonsmokers. As David Krogh describes it in his treatise *Smoking: The Artificial Passion,* psychologists have what they call "lie" tests in which they insert inarguable statements — "I do not always tell the truth" or "I am sometimes cold to my spouse" — and if test-takers consistently deny these statements, it is taken as evidence that they are not generally truthful. Smokers are much more truthful on these tests. "One theory," Krogh writes, "has it that their lack of deference and their surfeit of defiance combine to make them relatively indifferent to what people think of them."

These measures don't apply to all smokers, of course. But as general predictors of smoking behavior they are quite accurate, and the more someone smokes, the higher the likelihood that he or she fits this profile. "In the scientific spirit," Krogh writes, "I would invite readers to demonstrate [the smoking personality connection] to themselves by performing the following experiment. Arrange to go to a relaxed gathering of actors, rock musicians, or hairdressers on the one hand, or civil engineers, electricians, or computer programmers on the other, and observe how much smoking is going on. If your experience is anything like mine, the differences should be dramatic."

Here is another of the responses to my questionnaire. Can the extroverted personality be any clearer?

My grandfather was the only person around me when I was very little who smoked. He was a great Runyonesque figure, a trickster hero, who immigrated from Poland when he was a boy and who worked most of his life as a glazier. My mother used to like to say that when she was first brought to dinner with him she thought he might at any moment whisk the tablecloth off the table, leaving the settings there, just to amuse the crowd.

The significance of the smoking personality, I think, cannot be overstated. If you bundle all of these extroverts' traits together — defiance, sexual precocity, honesty, impulsiveness, indifference to the opinion of others, sensation seeking — you come up with an almost perfect definition of the kind of person many adolescents are drawn to. Maggie the au pair, and Pam P. on the school bus and Billy G. with his Grateful Dead records were all deeply cool people. But they weren't cool because they smoked. They smoked because they were cool. The very same character traits of rebelliousness and impulsivity and risk-taking and indifference to the opinion of others and precocity that made them so compelling to their adolescent peers also make it almost inevitable that they would also be drawn to the ultimate expression of adolescent rebellion, risk-taking, impulsivity, indifference to others, and precocity: the cigarette. This may seem like a simple point. But it is absolutely essential in understanding why the war on smoking has stumbled so badly. Over the past decade, the anti-smoking movement has railed against the tobacco companies for making smoking cool and has spent untold millions of dollars of public money trying to convince teenagers that smoking isn't cool. But that's not the point. Smoking was never cool. *Smokers* are cool. Smoking epidemics begin in precisely the same way that the suicide epidemic in Micronesia began or word-of-mouth epidemics begin or the AIDS epidemic began, because of the extraordinary influence of Pam P. and Billy G. and Maggie and their equivalents — the smoking versions of R. and Tom Gau and Gaetan Dugas. In this epidemic, as in all others, a very small group — a select few — are responsible for driving the epidemic forward.

4.

The teen smoking epidemic does not simply illustrate the Law of the Few, however. It is also a very good illustration of the Stickiness Factor. After all, the fact that overwhelming numbers of teenagers experiment with cigarettes as a result of their contacts with other teenagers is not, in and of itself, all that scary. The problem — the fact that has turned smoking into public health enemy number one — is that many of those teenagers end up continuing their cigarette experiment until they get hooked. The smoking experience is so memorable and powerful for some people that they cannot stop smoking. The habit sticks.

It is important to keep these two concepts — contagiousness and stickiness — separate, because they follow very different patterns and suggest very different strategies. Lois Weisberg is a contagious person. She knows so many people and belongs to so many worlds that she is able to spread a piece of information or an idea a thousand different ways, all at once. Lester Wunderman and the creators of *Blue's Clues,* on the other hand, are specialists in stickiness: they have a genius for creating messages that are memorable and that change people's behavior. Contagiousness is in larger part a function of the messenger. Stickiness is primarily a property of the message.

Smoking is no different. Whether a teenager picks up the habit depends on whether he or she has contact with one of those Salesmen who give teenagers "permission" to engage in deviant acts. But whether a teenager likes cigarettes enough to keep using them depends on a very different set of criteria. In a recent University of Michigan study, for example, a large group of people were polled about how they felt when they smoked their first cigarette. "What we found is that for almost everyone their initial experience with tobacco was somewhat aversive," said Ovide Pomerleau, one of the researchers on the project. "But what sorted out the smokers-to-be from the never-again smokers is that the smokers-to-be derived some overall pleasure from the experience — like the feeling of a buzz or a heady pleasurable feeling." The numbers are striking. Of the people who experimented with cigarettes a few times and then never smoked again, only about a quarter got any sort of pleasant "high" from their first cigarette. Of the ex-smokers — people who smoked for a while but later managed to quit — about a third got a pleasurable buzz. Of people who were light smokers, about half remembered their first cigarette well. Of the heavy smokers, though, 78 percent remembered getting a good buzz from their first few puffs. The questions of how sticky smoking ends up being to any single person, in other words, depends a great deal on his or her own particular initial reaction to nicotine.

This is a critical point, and one that is often lost in the heated rhetoric of the war on smoking. The tobacco industry, for instance, has been pilloried for years for denying that nicotine is addictive. That position, of course, is ridiculous. But the opposite notion often put forth by antismoking advocates — that nicotine is a deadly taskmaster that enslaves all who come in contact with it — is equally ridiculous. Of all the teenagers who experiment with cigarettes, only about a third ever go on to smoke regularly. Nicotine may be highly addictive, but it is only addictive in some people, some of the time. More important, it turns out that even among those who smoke regularly, there are enormous differences in the stickiness of their habit. Smoking experts used to think that 90 to 95 percent of all those who smoked were regular smokers. But several years ago, the smoking questions on the federal government's national health survey were made more specific, and researchers discovered, to their astonishment, that a fifth of all smokers don't smoke every day. There are millions of Americans, in other words, who manage to smoke regularly and not be hooked — people for whom smoking is contagious but not sticky. In the past few years, these "chippers" — as they have been dubbed — have been exhaustively studied, with the bulk of the work being done by University of Pittsburgh psychologist Saul Shiffman. Shiffman's definition of a chipper is someone who smokes no more than five cigarettes a day but who smokes at least four days a week. As Shiffman writes:

Chippers' smoking varies considerably from day to day, and their smoking patterns often include days of complete abstinence. Chippers reported little difficulty maintaining such casual abstinence and reportedly experienced almost no withdrawal symptoms when abstaining from smoking. . . . Unlike regular smokers who smoke soon on waking to replenish the nicotine that has cleared overnight, chippers go several hours before smoking their first cigarette of the day. In short, every indicator examined suggests that chippers are not addicted to nicotine and that their smoking is not driven by withdrawal relief or withdrawal avoidance.

Shiffman calls chippers the equivalent of social drinkers. They are people in control of their habit. He says:

Most of these people had never been heavy smokers. I think of them as developmentally retarded. Every smoker starts out as a chipper, in the early period, but then graduates more heavily into more dependent smoking. When we collected data about the early period of smoking, the chippers look like everyone else when they start out. The difference is that over time, the heavy smokers escalated whereas the chippers stayed where they were.

What distinguishes chippers from hard-core smokers? Probably genetic factors. Allan Collins of the University of Colorado, for example, recently took several groups of different strains of mice and injected each with steadily increasing amounts of nicotine. When nicotine reaches toxic levels in a mouse (nicotine is, after all, a poison) it has a seizure — its tail goes rigid; it begins running wildly around its cage; its head starts to jerk and snap; and eventually it flips over on its back. Collins wanted to see whether different strains of mice could handle different amounts of nicotine. Sure enough, they could. The strain of mice most tolerant of nicotine could handle about two to three times as much of the drug as the strain that had seizures at the lowest dose. "That's about in the same range as alcohol," Collins says. Then he put all the mice into cages and gave them two bottles to drink from: one filled with a simple saccharin solution, one filled with a saccharin solution laced with nicotine. This time he wanted to see whether there was any relationship between each strain's genetic tolerance to nicotine and the amount of nicotine they would voluntarily consume. Once again, there was. In fact, the correlation was almost perfect. The greater a mouse's genetic tolerance for nicotine, the more of the nicotine bottle it would drink. Collins thinks that there are genes in the brains of mice that govern how nicotine is processed — how quickly it causes toxicity, how much pleasure it gives, what kind of buzz it leaves — and that some strains of mice have genes that handle nicotine really well and extract the most pleasure from it and some have genes that treat nicotine like a poison.

Humans, obviously, aren't mice, and drinking nicotine from a bottle in a cage isn't the same as lighting up a Marlboro. But even if there is only a modest correlation between what goes on in mice brains and ours, these findings do seem to square with Pomerleau's study. The people who didn't get a buzz from their first cigarette and who found the whole experience so awful that they never smoked again are probably people whose bodies are acutely sensitive to nicotine, incapable of handling it in even the smallest doses. Chippers may be people who have the genes to derive pleasure from nicotine, but not the genes to handle it in large doses. Heavy smokers, meanwhile, may be people with the genes to do both. This is not to say that genes provide a total explanation for how much people smoke. Since nicotine is known to relieve boredom and stress, for example, people who are in boring or stressful situations are always going to smoke more than people who are not. It is simply to say that what makes smoking sticky is completely different from the kinds of things that make it contagious. If we are looking for Tipping Points in the war on smoking, then, we need to decide which of those sides of the epidemic we will have the most success attacking. Should we try to make smoking less contagious, to stop the Salesmen who spread the smoking virus? Or are we better off trying to make it less sticky, to look for ways to turn all smokers into chippers?

5.

Let's deal with the issue of contagion first. There are two possible strategies for stopping the spread of smoking. The first is to prevent the permission-givers — the Maggies and Billy G.'s — from smoking in the first place. This is clearly the most difficult path of all: the most independent, precocious, rebellious teens are hardly likely to be the most susceptible to rational health advice. The second possibility is to convince all those who look to people like Maggie and Billy G. for permission that they should look elsewhere, to get their cues as to what is cool, in this instance, from adults.

But this too is not easy. In fact, it may well be an even more difficult strategy than the first, for the simple reason that parents simply don't wield that kind of influence over children.

This is a hard fact to believe, of course. Parents are powerfully invested in the idea that they can shape their children's personalities and behavior. But, as Judith Harris brilliantly argued in her 1998 book *The Nurture Assumption*, the evidence for this belief is sorely lacking. Consider, for example, the results of efforts undertaken by psychologists over the years to try and measure this very question — the effect parents have on their children. Obviously, they pass on genes to their offspring, and genes play a big role in who we are. Parents provide love and affection in the early years of childhood; deprived of early emotional sustenance, children will be irreparably harmed. Parents provide food and a home and protection and the basics of everyday life that children need to be safe and healthy and happy. This much is easy. But does it make a lasting difference to the personality of your child if you are an anxious and inexperienced parent, as opposed to being authoritative and competent? Are you more likely to create intellectually curious children by filling your house with books? Does it affect your child's personality if you see him or her two hours a day, as opposed to eight hours a day? In other words, does the specific social environment that we create in our homes make a real difference in the way our children end up as adults? In a series of large and well-designed studies of twins — particularly twins separated at birth and reared apart —

geneticists have shown that most of the character traits that make us who we are — friendliness, extroversion, nervousness, openness, and so on — are about half determined by our genes and half determined by our environment, and the assumption has always been that this environment that makes such a big difference in our lives is the environment of the home. The problem is, however, that whenever psychologists have set out to look for this nurture effect, they can't find it.

One of the largest and most rigorous studies of this kind, for example, is known as the Colorado Adoption Project. In the mid-1970s, a group of researchers at the University of Colorado led by Robert Plomin, one of the world's leading behavioral geneticists, recruited 245 pregnant women from the Denver area who were about to give up their children for adoption. They then followed the children into their new homes, giving them a battery of personality and intelligence tests at regular intervals throughout their childhood and giving the same sets of tests to their adoptive parents. For the sake of comparison, the group also ran the same set of tests on a similar group of 245 parents and their biological children. For this comparison group, the results came out pretty much as one might expect. On things like measures of intellectual ability and certain aspects of personality, the biological children are fairly similar to their parents. For the adopted kids, however, the results are downright strange. Their scores have nothing whatsoever in common with their adoptive parents: these children are no more similar in their personality or intellectual skills to the people who raised them, fed them, clothed them, read to them, taught them, and loved them for sixteen years than they are to any two adults taken at random off the street.

This is, if you think about it, a rather extraordinary finding. Most of us believe that we are like our parents because of some combination of genes and, more important, of nurture — that parents, to a large extent, raise us in their own image. But if that is the case, if nurture matters so much, then why did the adopted kids not resemble their adoptive parents *at all*? The Colorado study isn't saying that genes explain everything and that environment doesn't matter. On the contrary, all of the results strongly suggest that our environment plays as big — if not bigger — a role as heredity in shaping personality and intelligence. What it is saying is that whatever that environmental influence is, it doesn't have a lot to do with parents. It's something else, and what Judith Harris argues is that that something else is the influence of peers.

Why, Harris asks, do the children of recent immigrants almost never retain the accent of their parents? How is it the children of deaf parents manage to learn how to speak as well and as quickly as children whose parents speak to them from the day they were born? The answer has always been that language is a skill acquired laterally — that what children pick up from other children is as, or more, important in the acquisition of language as what they pick up at home. What Harris argues is that this is also true more generally, that the environmental influence that helps children become who they are — that shapes their character and personality — is their peer group.

This argument has, understandably, sparked a great deal of controversy in the popular press. There are legitimate arguments about where — and how far — it can be applied. But there's no question that it has a great deal of relevance to the teenage smoking issue. The children of smokers are more than twice as likely to smoke as the children of nonsmokers. That's a well-known fact. But — to follow Harris's logic — that does not mean that parents who smoke around their children set an example that their kids follow. It simply means that smokers' children have inherited genes from their parents that predispose them toward nicotine addiction. Indeed studies of adopted children have shown that those raised by smokers are no more likely to end up as smokers themselves than those raised by nonsmokers. "In other words, effects of rearing variation (e.g. parents' lighting up or not, or having cigarettes in the home or not) were essentially nil by the time the children reached adulthood," the psychologist David Rowe writes in his 1994 book summarizing research on the question, *The Limits of Family Influence.* "The role of parents is a passive one — providing a set of genes at loci relevant to smoking risk, but not socially influencing their offspring."

To Rowe and Harris, the process by which teens get infected with the smoking habit is entirely bound up in the peer group. It's not about mimicking adult behavior, which is why teenage smoking is rising at a time when adult smoking is falling. Teenage smoking is about being a teenager, about sharing in the emotional experience and expressive language and rituals of adolescence, which are as impenetrable and irrational to outsiders as the rituals of adolescent suicide in Micronesia. How, under the circumstances, can we expect any adult intervention to make an impact?

"Telling teenagers about the health risks of smoking — It will make you wrinkled! It will make you impotent! It will make you dead! — is useless," Harris concludes. "This is adult propaganda; these are adult arguments. It is because adults don't approve of smoking — because there is something dangerous and disreputable about it — that teenagers want to do it."

6.

If trying to thwart the efforts of Salesmen — if trying to intervene in the internal world of adolescents — doesn't seem like a particularly effective strategy against smoking, then what of stickiness? Here the search for Tipping Points is very different. We suspect, as I wrote previously, that one of the reasons some experimenters never smoke again and some turn into lifelong addicts is that human beings may have very different innate tolerances for nicotine. In a perfect world we would give heavy smokers a pill that lowered their tolerance to the level of, say, a chipper. That would be a wonderful way of stripping smoking of its stickiness. Unfortunately we don't know how to do that. What we do have is the nicotine patch, which delivers a slow and steady dose of nicotine so that smokers don't have to turn to the dangers of cigarettes to get their fix. That's an anti-sticky strategy that has helped millions of smokers. But it is fairly clear that the patch is far from perfect. The most exhilarating way for an addict to get his fix is in the form of a "hit" — a high dose delivered quickly, that overwhelms the senses. Heroin users don't put themselves on a heroin intravenous drip: they shoot up two or three or four times a day, injecting a huge dose all at once. Smokers, on a lesser scale, do the same. They get a jolt from a cigarette, then pause, then get another jolt. The patch, though, gives you a steady dose of the drug over the course of the day, which is a pretty boring way to ingest nicotine. The patch seems no more a Tipping Point in the fight against the smoking epidemic than SlimFast milkshakes are a Tipping Point in the fight against obesity. Is there a better candidate?

I think there are two possibilities. The first can be found in the correlation between smoking and depression, a link discovered only recently. In 1986, a study of psychiatric outpatients in Minnesota found that half of them smoked, a figure well above the national average. Two years later, Columbia University psychologist Alexander Glassman discovered that 60 percent of the heavy smokers he was studying as part of an entirely different research project had a history of major depression. He followed that up with a major study published in the *Journal of the American Medical Association* in 1990 of 3,200 randomly selected adults. Of those who had at some time in their lives been diagnosed with a major psychiatric disorder, 74 percent had smoked at some point, and 14 percent had quit smoking. Of those who had never been diagnosed with a psychiatric problem, 53 percent had smoked at some point in their life and 31 percent had managed to quit smoking. As psychiatric problems increase, the correlation with smoking grows stronger. About 80 percent of alcoholics smoke. Close to 90 percent of schizophrenics smoke. In one particularly chilling study, a group of British psychiatrists compared the smoking behavior of a group of twelve- to fifteen-year-olds with emotional and behavioral problems with a group of children of the same age in mainstream schools. Half of the troubled kids were already smoking more than 21 cigarettes a week, even at that young age, versus 10 percent of the kids in the mainstream schools. As overall smoking rates decline, in other words, the habit is becoming concentrated among the most troubled and marginal members of society.

There are a number of theories as to why smoking matches up so strongly with emotional problems. The first is that the same kinds of things that would make someone susceptible to the contagious effects of smoking — low self-esteem, say, or an unhealthy and unhappy home life — are also the kinds of things that contribute to depression. More tantalizing, though, is some preliminary evidence that the two problems might have the same genetic root. For example, depression is believed to be the result, at least in part, of a problem in the production of certain key brain chemicals, in particular the neurotransmitters known as serotonin, dopamine, and norepinephrine. These are the chemicals that regulate mood, that contribute to feelings of confidence and mastery and pleasure. Drugs like Zoloft and Prozac work because they prompt the brain to produce more serotonin: they compensate, in other words, for the deficit of serotonin that some depressed people suffer from. Nicotine appears to do exactly the same thing with the other two key neurotransmitters — dopamine and norepinephrine.

Those smokers who are depressed, in short, are essentially using tobacco as a cheap way of treating their own depression, of boosting the level of brain chemicals they need to function normally. This effect is strong enough that when smokers with a history of psychiatric problems give up cigarettes, they run a sizable risk of relapsing into depression. Here is stickiness with a vengeance: not only do some smokers find it hard to quit because they are addicted to nicotine, but also because without nicotine they run the risk of a debilitating psychiatric illness.

This is a sobering fact. But it also suggests that tobacco may have a critical vulnerability: if you can treat smokers for depression, you may be able to make their habit an awful lot easier to break. Sure enough, this turns out to be the case. In the mid-1980s, researchers at what is now the Glaxo Wellcome pharmaceutical firm were doing a big national trial of a new antidepressant called bupropion when, much to their surprise, they began getting reports about smoking from the field. "I started hearing that patients were saying things like, 'I no longer have the desire to smoke,' or 'I've cut down on the number of cigarettes I'm smoking,' or 'Cigarettes don't taste as good anymore,'" said Andrew Johnston, who heads the psychiatry division for the company. "You can imagine that someone in my position gets reports about everything, so I didn't put much stock in them. But I kept getting them. It was very unusual." This was in 1986, before the depression-smoking link was well understood, so the company was initially puzzled. But what they soon realized was that bupropion was functioning as a kind of nicotine substitute. "The dopamine that nicotine releases goes to the prefrontal cortex of the brain," explains Johnston. "That's the pleasure center of the brain. It's what people believe is responsible for the pleasure, the sense of well-being, associated with smoking, and that's one of the reasons it's so hard to quit. Nicotine also increases norepinephrine, and that's the reason that when you try to quit smoking and you no longer get so much norepinephrine, you get agitation and irritability. Bupropion does two things. It increases your dopamine, so smokers don't have the desire to smoke, then it replaces some of the norepinephrine, so they don't have the agitation, the withdrawal symptoms."

Glaxo Wellcome has tested the drug — now marketed under the name Zyban — in heavily addicted smokers (more than 15 cigarettes a day) and found remarkable effects. In the study, 23 percent of smokers given a course of anti-smoking counseling and a placebo quit after four weeks. Of those given counseling and the nicotine patch, 36 percent had quit after four weeks. The same figure for Zyban, though, was 49 percent, and of those heavily addicted smokers given both Zyban and the patch, 58 percent had quit after a month. Interestingly, Zoloft and Prozac — the serotonin drugs — don't seem to help smokers to quit. It's not enough to lift mood, in other words; you have to lift mood in precisely the same way that nicotine does, and only Zyban does that. This is not to say that it is a perfect drug. As with all smoking cessation aids, it has the least success with the heaviest smokers. But what the drug's initial success has proven is that it is possible to find a sticky Tipping Point with smoking: that by zeroing in on depression, you can exploit a critical vulnerability in the addiction process.

There is a second potential Tipping Point on the stickiness question that becomes apparent if you go back and look again at what happens to teens when they start smoking. In the beginning, when teens first experiment with cigarettes, they are all chippers. They smoke only occasionally. Most of those teens soon quit and never smoke again. A few continue to chip for many years afterward, without becoming addicted. About a third end up as regular smokers. What's interesting about this period, however, is that it takes about three years for the teens in that last group to go from casual to regular smoking — roughly from fifteen to eighteen years of age — and then for the next five to seven years there is a gradual escalation of their habit. "When someone in high school is smoking on a regular basis, he or she isn't smoking a pack a day," Neal Benowitz, an addiction expert at the University of California at San Francisco, says. "It takes until their twenties to get to that level."

Nicotine addiction, then, is far from an instant development. It takes time for most people to get hooked on cigarettes, and just because teens are smoking at fifteen doesn't mean that they will inevitably become addicted. You've got about three years to stop them. The second, even more intriguing implication of this, is that nicotine addiction isn't a linear phenomenon. It's not that if you need one cigarette a day you are a little bit addicted, and if you need two cigarettes a day you are a little bit more addicted, and if you need ten cigarettes you are ten times as addicted as when you needed one cigarette. It suggests, instead, that there is an addiction Tipping Point, a threshold — that if you smoke below a certain number of cigarettes you aren't addicted at all, but once you go above that magic number you suddenly are. This is another, more complete way of making sense of chippers: they are people who simply never smoke enough to hit that addiction threshold. A hardened smoker, on the other hand, is someone who, at some point, crosses that line.

What is the addiction threshold? Well, no one believes that it is exactly the same for all people. But Benowitz and Jack Henningfield — who are probably the leading nicotine experts in the world — have made some educated guesses. Chippers, they point out, are people who are capable of smoking up to five cigarettes a day without getting addicted. That suggests that the amount of nicotine found in five cigarettes — which works out to somewhere between four and six milligrams of nicotine — is probably somewhere close to the addiction threshold. What Henningfield and Benowitz suggest, then, is that tobacco companies be required to lower the level of nicotine so that even the heaviest smokers — those smoking, say, 30 cigarettes a day — could not get anything more than five milligrams of nicotine within a 24-hour period. That level, the two argued in an editorial in the prestigious *New England Journal of Medicine,* "should be adequate to prevent or limit the development of addiction in most young people. At the same time it may provide enough nicotine for taste and sensory stimulation." Teens, in other words, would continue to experiment with cigarettes for all the reasons that they have ever experimented with cigarettes —

because the habit is contagious, because cool kids are smoking, because they want to fit in. But, because of the reduction of nicotine levels below the addiction threshold, the habit would no longer be sticky. Cigarette smoking would be less like the flu and more like the common cold: easily caught but easily defeated.

It is important to put these two stickiness factors in perspective. The anti-smoking movement has focused, so far, on raising cigarette prices, curtailing cigarette advertising, running public health messages on radio and television, limiting access of cigarettes to minors, and drilling anti-tobacco messages into schoolchildren, and in the period that this broad, seemingly comprehensive, ambitious campaign has been waged, teenage smoking has sky-rocketed. We've been obsessed with changing attitudes toward tobacco on a mass scale, but we haven't managed to reach the groups whose attitude needs to change the most. We've been obsessed with foiling the influence of smoking Salesmen. But the influence of those Salesmen increasingly looks like something we cannot break. We have, in short, somehow become convinced that we need to tackle the whole problem, all at once. But the truth is that we don't. We only need to find the stickiness Tipping Points, and those are the links to depression and the nicotine threshold.

The second lesson of the stickiness strategy is that it permits a more reasonable approach to teenage experimentation. The absolutist approach to fighting drugs proceeds on the premise that experimentation equals addiction. We don't want our children ever to be exposed to heroin or pot or cocaine because we think that the lure of these substances is so strong that even the smallest exposure will be all it takes. But do you know what the experimentation statistics are for illegal drugs? In the 1996 Household Survey on Drug Abuse, 1.1 percent of those polled said that they had used heroin at least once. But only 18 percent of that 1.1 percent had used it in the past year, and only 9 percent had used it in the past month. That is not the profile of a particularly sticky drug. The figures for cocaine are even more striking. Of those who have ever tried cocaine, less than one percent — 0.9 percent — are regular users. What these figures tell us is that experimentation and actual hard-core use are two entirely separate things — that for a drug to be contagious does not automatically mean that it is also sticky. In fact, the sheer number of people who appear to have tried cocaine at least once should tell us that the urge among teens to try something dangerous is pretty nearly universal. This is what teens do. This is how they learn about the world, and most of the time — in 99.1 percent of the cases with cocaine — that experimentation doesn't result in anything bad happening. We have to stop fighting this kind of experimentation. We have to accept it and even to embrace it. Teens are always going to be fascinated by people like Maggie the au pair and Billy G. and Pam P., and they should be fascinated by people like that, if only to get past the adolescent fantasy that to be rebellious and truculent and irresponsible is a good way to spend your life. What we should be doing instead of fighting experimentation is making sure that experimentation doesn't have serious consequences.

I think it is worth repeating something from the beginning of this chapter, a quote from Donald Rubinstein describing just how deeply embedded suicide had become in the teen culture of Micronesia.

> A number of young boys who attempted suicide reported that they first saw or heard about it when they were 8 or 10 years old. Their suicide attempts appear in the spirit of imitative or experimental play. One 11-year-old boy, for example, hanged himself inside his house and when found he was already unconscious and his tongue protruding. He later explained that he wanted to "try" out hanging. He said that he did not want to die.

What is tragic about this is not that these little boys were experimenting. Experimenting is what little boys do. What is tragic is that they have chosen to experiment with something that you cannot experiment with. Unfortunately, there isn't ever going to be a safer form of suicide, to help save the teenagers of Micronesia. But there can be a safer form of smoking, and by paying attention to the Tipping Points of the addiction process we can make that safer, less sticky form of smoking possible.

EIGHT

Conclusion

FOCUS, TEST, AND BELIEVE

N ot long ago a nurse by the name of Georgia Sadler began a campaign to increase knowledge and awareness of diabetes and breast cancer in the black community of San Diego. She wanted to create a grassroots movement toward prevention, and so she began setting up seminars in black churches around the city. The results, however, were disappointing. "There'd be maybe two hundred people in church, but we'd get only twenty or so to stay, and the people who were staying were people who already knew a lot about those diseases and just wanted to know more. It was very discouraging." Sadler couldn't get her message to tip outside of that small group.

She realized she needed a new context. "I guess people were tired and hungry after the service," she says. "We all have a busy life. People wanted to get home." She needed a place where women were relaxed, receptive to new ideas, and had the time and opportunity to hear something new.

She also needed a new messenger, someone who was a little bit Connector, a little bit Salesman, and a little bit Maven. She needed a new, stickier way of presenting the information. And she needed to make all those changes in such a way that she didn't exceed the very small amount of money she'd cobbled together from various foundations and funding groups. Her solution? Move the campaign from black churches to beauty salons.

"It's a captive audience," Sadler says. "These women may be at a salon for anywhere from two hours to eight hours, if they're having their hair braided." The stylist also enjoys a special relationship with her client. "Once you find someone who can manage your hair, you'll drive a hundred miles to see her. The stylist is your friend. She takes you through your high school graduation, your wedding, your first baby. It's a long-term relationship. It's a trusting relationship. You literally and figuratively let your hair down in a salon." There is something about the profession of stylist, as well, that seems to attract a certain kind of person — someone who communicates easily and well with others, someone with a wide variety of acquaintances. "They're natural conversationalists," Sadler says. "They love talking to you. They tend to be very intuitive, because they have to keep an eye on you and see how you're doing."

She gathered together a group of stylists from the city for a series of training sessions. She brought in a folklorist to help coach the stylists in how to present their information about breast cancer in a compelling manner. "We wanted to rely on traditional methods of communication," Sadler says. "This isn't a classroom setting. We wanted this to be something that women wanted to share, that they wanted to pass on. And how much easier is it to hang the hooks of knowledge on a story?" Sadler kept a constant cycle of new information and gossipy tidbits and conversational starters about breast cancer flowing into the salons, so that each time a client came back, the stylist could seize on some new cue to start a conversation. She wrote the material up in large print, and put it on laminated sheets that would survive the rough and tumble of a busy hair salon. She set up an evaluation program to find out what was working and to see how successful she was in changing attitudes and getting women to have mammograms and diabetes tests, and what she found out was that her program worked. It is possible to do a lot with a little.

Over the course of *The Tipping Point* we've looked at a number of stories like this — from the battle against crime in New York to Lester Wunderman's Columbia Record Club treasure hunt — and what they all have in common is their modesty. Sadler didn't go to the National Cancer Institute or the California State Department of Health and ask for millions of dollars to run some elaborate, multimedia public awareness campaign. She didn't go door to door through the neighborhoods of San Diego, signing women up for free mammograms. She didn't bombard the airwaves with a persistent call for prevention and testing. Instead she took the small budget that she had and thought about how to use it more intelligently. She changed the context of her message. She changed the messenger, and she changed the message itself. She focused her efforts.

This is the first lesson of the Tipping Point. Starting epidemics requires concentrating resources on a few key areas. The Law of the Few says that Connectors, Mavens, and Salesmen are responsible for starting word-of-mouth epidemics, which means that if you are interested in starting a word-of-mouth epidemic, your resources ought to be solely concentrated on those three groups. No one else matters. Telling William Dawes that the British were coming did nothing for the colonists of New England. But telling Paul Revere ultimately meant the difference between defeat and victory. The creators of *Blue's Clues* developed a sophisticated, half-hour television show that children loved. But they realized that there was no way that children could remember and learn everything they needed to remember and learn from a single viewing. So they did what no one had ever done in television before. They ran the same show five times in a row. Sadler didn't try to reach every woman in San Diego all at once. She took what resources she had and put them all into one critical place — the beauty salon.

A critic looking at these tightly focused, targeted interventions might dismiss them as Band-Aid solutions. But that phrase should not be considered a term of disparagement. The Band-Aid is an inexpensive, convenient, and remarkably versatile solution to an astonishing array of problems. In their history, Band-Aids have probably allowed millions of people to keep working or playing tennis or cooking or walking when they would otherwise have had to stop. The Band-Aid solution is actually the best kind of solution because it involves solving a problem with the minimum amount of effort and time and cost. We have, of course, an instinctive disdain for this kind of solution because there is something in all of us that feels that true answers to problems have to be comprehensive, that there is virtue in the dogged and indiscriminate application of effort, that slow and steady should win the race. The problem, of course, is that the indiscriminate application of effort is something that is not always possible. There are times when we need a convenient shortcut, a way to make a lot out of a little, and that is what Tipping Points, in the end, are all about.

The theory of Tipping Points requires, however, that we reframe the way we think about the world. I have spent a lot of time, in this book, talking about the idiosyncrasies of the way we relate to new information and to each other. We have trouble estimating dramatic, exponential change. We cannot conceive that a piece of paper folded over 50 times could reach the sun. There are abrupt limits to the number of cognitive categories we can make and the number of people we can truly love and the number of acquaintances we can truly know. We throw up our hands at a problem phrased in an abstract way, but have no difficulty at all solving the same problem rephrased as a social dilemma. All of these things are expressions of the peculiarities of the human mind and heart, a refutation of the notion that the way we function and communicate and process information is straightforward and transparent. It is not. It is messy and opaque. *Sesame Street* and *Blue's Clues* succeed, in large part, because of things they do that are not obvious. Who would have known, beforehand, that Big Bird had to be on the same set as the adult characters? Or who could have predicted that going from 100 to 150 workers in a plant isn't a problem, but going from 150 to 200 is a huge problem? In the phone book names test that I gave, I'm not sure anyone would have predicted that the high scores would have been over 100 and the low scores under 10. We think people are different, but not that different.

The world — much as we want it to — does not accord with our intuition. This is the second lesson of the Tipping Point. Those who are successful at creating social epidemics do not just do what they think is right. They deliberately test their intuitions. Without the evidence of the Distracter, which told them that their intuition about fantasy and reality was wrong, *Sesame Street* would today be a forgotten footnote in television history. Lester Wunderman's gold box sounded like a silly idea until he proved how much more effective it was than conventional advertising. That no one responded to Kitty Genovese's screams sounded like an open-and-shut case of human indifference, until careful psychological testing demonstrated the powerful influence of context. To make sense of social epidemics, we must first understand that human communication has its own set of very unusual and counterintuitive rules.

What must underlie successful epidemics, in the end, is a bedrock belief that change is possible, that people can radically transform their behavior or beliefs in the face of the right kind of impetus. This, too, contradicts some of the most ingrained assumptions we hold about ourselves and each other. We like to think of ourselves as autonomous and inner-directed, that who we are and how we act is something permanently set by our genes and our temperament. But if you add up the examples of Salesmen and Connectors, of Paul Revere's ride and *Blue's Clues*, and the Rule of 150 and the New York subway cleanup and the Fundamental Attribution Error, they amount to a very different conclusion about what it means to be human. We are actually powerfully influenced by our surroundings, our immediate context, and the personalities of those around us. Taking the graffiti off the walls of New York's subways turned New Yorkers into better citizens. Telling seminarians to hurry turned them into bad citizens. The suicide of a charismatic young Micronesian set off an epidemic of suicides that lasted for a decade. Putting a little gold box in the corner of a Columbia Record Club advertisement suddenly made record buying by mail seem irresistible. To look closely at complex behaviors like smoking or suicide or crime is to appreciate how suggestible we are in the face of what we see and hear, and how acutely sensitive we are to even the smallest details of everyday life. That's why social change is so volatile and so often inexplicable, because it is the nature of all of us to be volatile and inexplicable.

But if there is difficulty and volatility in the world of the Tipping Point, there is a large measure of hopefulness as well. Merely by manipulating the size of a group, we can dramatically improve its receptivity to new ideas. By tinkering with the presentation of information, we can significantly improve its stickiness. Simply by finding and reaching those few special people who hold so much social power, we can shape the course of social epidemics. In the end, Tipping Points are a reaffirmation of the potential for change and the power of intelligent action. Look at the world around you. It may seem like an immovable, implacable place. It is not. With the slightest push — in just the right place — it can be tipped.

Endnotes

Page 5.
For a good summary of New York City crime statistics, see: Michael Massing, "The Blue Revolution," in the *New York Review of Books*, November 19, 1998, pp. 32–34. There is another good discussion of the anomalous nature of the New York crime drop in William Bratton and William Andrews, "What We've Learned About Policing," in *City Journal*, Spring 1999, p. 25.

Page 10.
The leader in research on yawning is Robert Provine, a psychologist at the University of Maryland. Among his papers on the subject are:

Robert Provine, "Yawning as a Stereotyped Action Pattern and Releasing Stimulus," *Ethology* (1983), vol. 72, pp. 109–122.

Robert Provine, "Contagious Yawning and Infant Imitation," *Bulletin of the Psychonomic Society* (1989), vol. 27, no. 2, pp. 125–126.

Page 12.
The best way to understand the Tipping Point is to imagine a hypothetical outbreak of the flu. Suppose, for example, that one summer 1,000 tourists come to Manhattan from Canada carrying an untreatable strain of twenty-four-hour virus. This strain of flu has a 2 percent infection rate, which is to say that one out of every 50 people who come into close contact with someone carrying it catches the bug himself. Let's say that 50 is also exactly the number of people the average Manhattanite — in the course of riding the subways and mingling with colleagues at work — comes into contact with every day. What we have, then, is a disease in equilibrium. Those 1,000 Canadian tourists pass on the virus to 1,000 new people on the day they arrive. And the next day those 1,000 newly infected people pass on the virus to another 1,000 people, just as the original 1,000 tourists who started the epidemic are returning to health. With those getting sick and those getting well so perfectly in balance, the flu chugs along at a steady but unspectacular clip through the rest of the summer and the fall.

But then comes the Christmas season. The subways and buses get more crowded with tourists and shoppers, and instead of running into an even 50 people a day, the average Manhattanite now has close contact with, say, 55 people a day. All of a sudden, the equilibrium is disrupted. The 1,000 flu carriers now run into 55,000 people a day, and at a 2 percent infection rate, that translates into 1,100 cases the following day. Those 1,100, in turn, are now passing on their virus to 55,000 people as well, so that by day three there are 1,210 Manhattanites with the flu and by day four 1,331 and by the end of the week there are nearly 2,000, and so on up, in an exponential spiral, until Manhattan has a full-blown flu epidemic on its hands by Christmas Day. That moment when the average flu carrier went from running into 50 people a day to running into 55 people was the Tipping Point. It was the point at which an ordinary and stable phenomenon — a low-level flu outbreak — turned into a public health crisis. If you were to draw a graph of the progress of the Canadian flu epidemic, the Tipping Point would be the point on the graph where the line suddenly turned upward.

Tipping Points are moments of great sensitivity. Changes made right at the Tipping Point can have enormous consequences. Our Canadian flu became an epidemic when the number of New Yorkers running into a flu carrier jumped from 50 to 55 a day. But had that same small change happened in the opposite direction, if the number had dropped from 50 to 45, that change would have pushed the number of flu victims down to 478 within a week, and within a few weeks more at that rate, the Canadian flu would have vanished from Manhattan entirely. Cutting the number exposed from 70 to 65, or 65 to 60 or 60 to 55 would not have been sufficient to end the epidemic. But a change right at the Tipping Point, from 50 to 45, would.

The Tipping Point model has been described in several classic works of sociology. I suggest:

Mark Granovetter, "Threshold Models of Collective Behavior," *American Journal of Sociology* (1978), vol. 83, pp. 1420–1443.

Mark Granovetter and R. Soong, "Threshold Models of Diffusion and Collective Behavior," *Journal of Mathematical Sociology* (1983), vol. 9, pp. 165–179.

Thomas Schelling, "Dynamic Models of Segregation," *Journal of Mathematical Sociology* (1971), vol. 1, pp. 143–186.

Thomas Schelling, *Micromotives and Macrobehavior* (New York: W. W. Norton, 1978).

Jonathan Crane, "The Epidemic Theory of Ghettos and Neighborhood Effects on Dropping Out and Teenage Childbearing," *American Journal of Sociology* (1989), vol. 95, no. 5, pp. 1226–1259.

CHAPTER ONE: THE THREE RULES OF EPIDEMICS

Page 15.
One of the best lay treatments of the mechanics of a disease epidemic is Gabriel Rotello, *Sexual Ecology: AIDS and the Destiny of Gay Men* (New York: Penguin Books, 1997).

The Centers for Disease Control's explanation for the Baltimore syphilis epidemic can be found in the *Mortality and Morbidity Weekly*

Report, "Outbreak of Primary and Secondary Syphilis — Baltimore City, Maryland, 1995," March 1, 1996.

Page 19.
Richard Koch, *The 80/20 Principle: The Art of Achieving More with Less* (New York: Bantam, 1998).

John Potteratt, "Gonorrhea as a social disease," *Sexually Transmitted Disease* (1985), vol. 12, no. 25.

Page 21.
Randy Shilts, *And the Band Played On* (New York: St. Martin's Press, 1987).

Page 22.
Jaap Goudsmit, *Viral Sex: The Nature of AIDS* (New York: Oxford Press, 1997), pp. 25–37.

Page 25.
Richard Kluger, *Ashes to Ashes* (New York: Alfred A. Knopf, 1996), pp. 158–159.

Page 27.
A. M. Rosenthal, *Thirty-Eight Witnesses* (New York: McGraw-Hill, 1964).

Page 28.
John Darley and Bibb Latane, "Bystander Intervention in Emergencies: Diffusion of Responsibility," *Journal of Personality and Social Psychology* (1968), vol. 8, pp. 377–383.

CHAPTER TWO: THE LAW OF THE FEW

Page 30.
All discussion of Paul Revere comes from the remarkable book by David Hackett Fischer, *Paul Revere's Ride* (New York: Oxford University Press, 1994).

Page 34.
Stanley Milgram, "The Small World Problem," *Psychology Today* (1967), vol. 1, pp. 60–67. For a (highly) theoretical treatment of the small-world subject, see: Manfred Kochen (ed.), *The Small World* (Norwood, New Jersey: Ablex Publishing Corp., 1989).

Page 35.
Carol Werner and Pat Parmelee, "Similarity of Activity Preferences Among Friends: Those Who Play Together Stay Together," *Social Psychology Quarterly* (1979), vol. 42, no. 1, pp. 62–66.

Page 47.

Brett Tjaden's project, now maintained by the University of Virginia computer science department, is called the Oracle of Bacon at Virginia and can be found at www.cs.virginia.edu/oracle/.

Page 53.

Mark Granovetter, *Getting a Job* (Chicago: University of Chicago Press, 1995).

Page 60.

The supermarket promotion work is described in: J. Jeffrey Inman, Leigh McAlister, and Wayne D. Hoyer, "Promotion Signal: Proxy for a Price Cut?" *Journal of Consumer Research* (1990), vol. 17, pp. 74–81.

Page 61.

Linda Price and colleagues have written a number of explorations of the Market Maven phenomenon, among them:

Lawrence F. Feick and Linda L. Price, "The Market Maven: A Diffuser of Marketplace Information," *Journal of Marketing* (January 1987), vol. 51, pp. 83–97.

Robin A. Higie, Lawrence F. Feick, and Linda L. Price, "Types and Amount of Word-of-Mouth Communications About Retailers," *Journal of Retailing* (Fall 1987), vol. 63, no. 3, pp. 260–278.

Linda L. Price, Lawrence F. Feick, and Audrey Guskey, "Everyday Market Helping Behavior," *Journal of Public Policy and Marketing* (Fall 1995), vol. 14, no. 2, pp. 255–266.

Page 74.

Brian Mullen et al., "Newscasters' facial expressions and voting behavior of viewers: Can a smile elect a President?" *Journal of Personality and Social Psychology* (1986), vol. 51, pp. 291–295.

Page 77.

Gary L. Wells and Richard E. Petty, "The Effects of Overt Head Movements on Persuasion," *Basic and Applied Social Psychology* (1980), vol. 1, no. 3, pp. 219–230.

Page 81.

William S. Condon, "Cultural Microrhythms," in M. Davis (ed.), *Interaction Rhythms: Periodicity in Communicative Behavior* (New York: Human Sciences Press, 1982), pp. 53–76.

Page 84.

Elaine Hatfield, John T. Cacioppo, and Richard L. Rapson, *Emotional Contagion* (Cambridge: Cambridge University Press, 1994).

Page 85.

Howard Friedman et al., "Understanding and Assessing Nonverbal Expressiveness: The Affective Communication Test," *Journal of Personality and Social Psychology* (1980), vol. 39, no. 2, pp. 333–351.

Howard Friedman and Ronald Riggio, "Effect of Individual Differences in Nonverbal Expressiveness on Transmission of Emotion," *Journal of Nonverbal Behavior* (Winter 1981), vol. 6, pp. 96–104.

CHAPTER THREE: THE STICKINESS FACTOR

Page 89.
The best history of *Sesame Street* is probably: Gerald Lesser, *Children and Television: Lessons from Sesame Street* (New York: Vintage Books, 1975).
See also Jim Henson, *The Works: The Art, the Magic, the Imagination* (New York: Random House, 1993).

Page 91.
Virtually every time *Sesame Street*'s educational value has been tested — and the show has been subject to more academic scrutiny than any television show in history — it has been proved to improve the reading and learning skills of its viewers. Most recently, a group of researchers at the University of Massachusetts and the University of Kansas went back and recontacted close to 600 children whose television watching as preschoolers they had tracked back in the 1980s. The kids were now all in high school, and the researchers found — to their astonishment — that the kids who had watched *Sesame Street* the most as four- and five-year-olds were still doing better in school than those who didn't. Even after controlling for things like parent's education, family size, and preschool vocabulary level, the *Sesame Street* watchers did better in high school in English, math, and science and they were also much more likely to read books for leisure than those who didn't watch the show, or who watched the show less. According to the study, for every hour per week of *Sesame Street* viewing, high-school grade point averages increased by .052, which means that a child who watched five hours of *Sesame Street* a week at age five was earning, on average, about one quarter of a grade level higher than a child of similar background who never watched the show. Somehow a single television show an hour long, watched over the course of no more than two or three years, was still making a difference twelve and fifteen years later.

This research is summarized in "Effects of Early Childhood Media Use on Adolescent Achievement" by the "Recontact" Project of the University of Massachusetts at Amherst and the University of Kansas, Lawrence (1995).

See also: John C. Wright and Aletha C. Huston, "Effects of educational TV viewing of lower income preschoolers on academic skills, school readiness, and school adjustment one to three years later," *A Report to Children's Television Workshop*, University of Kansas (1995).

Page 93.
Lester Wunderman has written a perfectly wonderful autobiography that tells the story of Columbia Record House and many other tales of direct marketing.

Lester Wunderman, *Being Direct: Making Advertising Pay* (New York: Random House, 1996), chapters 10 and 11.

Page 96.
Howard Levanthal, Robert Singer, and Susan Jones, "Effects on Fear and Specificity of Recommendation Upon Attitudes and Behavior," *Journal of Personality and Social Psychology* (1965), vol. 2, no. 1, pp. 20–29.

Page 100.
The best summary of the "active" theory of television watching is:

Daniel Anderson and Elizabeth Lorch, "Looking at Television: Action or Reaction?" in *Children's Understanding of Television: Research on Attention and Comprehension* (New York: Academic Press, 1983).

Page 102.
Palmer's work is written up in a number of places. For example: Edward Palmer, "Formative Research in Educational Television Production: The Experience of CTW," in W. Schramm (ed.), *Quality in Instructional Television* (Honolulu: University Press of Hawaii, 1972), pp. 165–187.

Page 108.
Barbara Flagg's eye movement research on "Oscar's Blending" and "Hug" is summarized in Barbara N. Flagg, "Formative Evaluation of *Sesame Street* Using Eye Movement Photography," in J. Baggaley (ed.), *Experimental Research in Televised Instruction*, vol. 5 (Montreal, Canada: Concordia Research, 1982).

Page 115.
Ellen Markman, *Categorization and Naming in Children* (Cambridge: MIT Press, 1989).

Page 118.
Nelson, Katherine (ed.), *Narratives from the Crib* (Cambridge: Harvard University Press, 1989). See essays by Bruner and Lucariello, and Feldman.

CHAPTER FOUR: THE POWER OF CONTEXT (PART ONE)

Page 133.
The best accounts of the Goetz shooting can be found in: George P. Fletcher, *A Crime of Self Defense* (New York: Free Press, 1988).

Also: Lillian Rubin, *Quiet Rage: Bernie Goetz in a Time of Madness* (New York: Farrar, Straus and Giroux, 1986).

Page 136.
For a good summary of New York City crime statistics see: Michael Massing, "The Blue Revolution," in *New York Review of Books,* November 19, 1998, pp. 32–34.

William Bratton, *Turnaround: How America's Top Cop Reversed the Crime Epidemic* (New York: Random House, 1998), p. 141.

Page 140.
Malcolm Gladwell, "The Tipping Point," *The New Yorker,* June 3, 1996, pp. 32–39. This article is archived at www.gladwell.com. There is another good discussion of the anomalous nature of the New York crime drop in William Bratton and William Andrews, "What We've Learned About Policing," in *City Journal,* Spring 1999, p. 25.

Page 141.
George L. Kelling and Catherine M. Coles, *Fixing Broken Windows* (New York: Touchstone, 1996), p. 20.

Page 152.
The description of the Zimbardo experiments comes from Craig Haney, Curtis Banks, and Philip Zimbardo, "Interpersonal Dynamics in a Simulated Prison," *International Journal of Criminology and Penology* (1973), no. 1, p. 73. The quotes from guards and Zimbardo come from *CBS 60 Minutes,* August 30, 1998, "The Stanford Prison Experiment."

Page 155.
For a good summary of the cheating experiments on schoolchildren, see: Hugh Hartshorne and Mark May, "Studies in the Organization of Character," in H. Munsinger (ed.), *Readings in Child Development* (New York: Holt, Rinehart and Winston, 1971), pp. 190–197.

Their complete findings can be found in Hugh Hartshorne and Mark May, *Studies in the Nature of Character,* vol. 1, *Studies in Deceit* (New York: Macmillan, 1928).

Page 159.
The vervet and card-game work is described in Robin Dunbar, *The Trouble with Science* (Cambridge: Harvard University Press, 1995), chapters six and seven.

Page 160.
The FAE is summarized in Richard E. Nisbett and Lee Ross, *The Person and the Situation* (Philadelphia: Temple University Press, 1991).

The quiz game experiment is described in: "Lee D. Ross, Teresa M. Amabile, and Julia L. Steinmetz, "Social Roles, Social Control, and Biases in Social-Perception Process," *Journal of Personality and Social Psychology* (1977), vol. 35, no. 7, pp. 485–494.

Page 161.
The birth order myth is brilliantly dissected in Judith Rich Harris, *The Nurture Assumption* (New York: Free Press, 1998), p. 365.

Page 162.
Walter Mischel, "Continuity and Change in Personality," *American Psychologist* (1969), vol. 24, pp. 1012–1017.

Page 163.
John Darley and Daniel Batson, "From Jerusalem to Jericho: A study of situational and dispositional variables in helping behavior," *Journal of Personality and Social Psychology* (1973), vol. 27, pp. 100–119.

Page 168.
Myra Friedman, "My Neighbor Bernie Goetz," *New York*, February 18, 1985, pp. 35–41.

CHAPTER FIVE: THE POWER OF CONTEXT (PART TWO)

Page 176.
George A. Miller, "The Magical Number Seven," *Psychological Review* (March 1956), vol. 63, no. 2.

C. J. Buys and K. L. Larsen, "Human Sympathy Groups," *Psychology Reports* (1979), vol. 45, pp. 547–553.

Page 177.
S. L. Washburn and R. Moore, *Ape into Man* (Boston: Little, Brown, 1973).

Dunbar's theories have been described in a number of places. The best academic summary is probably: R. I. M. Dunbar, "Neocortex size as a constraint on group size in primates," *Journal of Human Evolution* (1992), vol. 20, pp. 469–493.

He has also written a marvelous work of popular science: Robin Dunbar, *Grooming, Gossip, and the Evolution of Language* (Cambridge: Harvard University Press, 1996).

Page 187.
Daniel Wegner, "Transactive Memory in Close Relationships," *Journal of Personality and Social Psychology* (1991), vol. 61, no. 6, pp. 923–929.

Another good discussion of the issue is: Daniel Wegner, "Transactive Memory: A Contemporary Analysis of the Group Mind," in Brian Mullen and George Goethals (eds.), *Theories of Group Behavior* (New York: Springer-Verlag, 1987), pp. 200–201.

CHAPTER SIX: CASE STUDY

Page 196.
Bruce Ryan and Neal Gross, "The Diffusion of Hybrid Seed Corn in Two Iowa Communities," *Rural Sociology* (1943), vol. 8, pp. 15–24.

The study is nicely described (along with other work on diffusion theory) in Everett Rogers, *Diffusion of Innovations* (New York: Free Press, 1995).

Page 197.

Geoffrey Moore, *Crossing the Chasm* (New York: HarperCollins, 1991), pp. 9–14.

Page 201.

Gordon Allport and Leo Postman, *The Psychology of Rumor* (New York: Henry Holt, 1947), pp. 135–158.

Page 204.

Thomas Valente, Robert K. Foreman, and Benjamin Junge, "Satellite Exchange in the Baltimore Needle Exchange Program," *Public Health Reports,* in press.

CHAPTER SEVEN: CASE STUDY

Page 216.

The story of Sima is beautifully told by the anthropologist Donald H. Rubinstein in several papers, among them: "Love and Suffering: Adolescent Socialization and Suicide in Micronesia," *Contemporary Pacific* (Spring 1995), vol. 7, no. 1, pp. 21–53.

Donald H. Rubinstein, "Epidemic Suicide Among Micronesian Adolescents," *Social Science and Medicine* (1983), vol. 17, p. 664.

Page 220.

W. Kip Viscusi, *Smoking: Making the Risky Decision* (New York: Oxford University Press, 1992), pp. 61–78.

Page 221.

These statistics on the teen smoking rise come from a number of sources, and they differ according to how "new smokers" are measured. According to a Centers for Disease Control study released in October of 1998, for example, the number of American youths — people under the age of 18 — taking up smoking as a daily habit increased from 708,000 in 1988 to 1.2 million in 1996, an increase of 73 percent. The rate at which teens became smokers also increased. In 1996, 77 out of every 1,000 nonsmoking teens picked up the habit. In 1988, the rate was 51 per 1,000. The highest rate ever recorded was 67 per 1,000 in 1977, and the lowest was 44 per 1,000 in 1983. ("New teen smokers up 73 percent": Associated Press, October 9, 1998.) It is also the case that smoking among college students — a slightly older cohort — is also on the rise. In this study by the Harvard School of Public Health — published in the *Journal of the American Medical Association,* November 18, 1998 — the statistic used was percentage of college students who had smoked at least one cigarette in the past 30 days. In 1993, the number was 22.3 percent. By 1997, it had increased to 28.5 percent.

Page 222.
David Phillips's first paper on suicide rates after news stories of celebrity suicides was: D. P. Phillips, "The Influence of Suggestion on Suicide: Substantive and Theoretical Implications of the Werther Effect," *American Sociological Review* (1974), vol. 39, pp. 340–354. A good summary of that paper — and the statistic about Marilyn Monroe — can be found at the beginning of his paper on traffic accidents, David P. Phillips, "Suicide, Motor Vehicle Fatalities, and the Mass Media: Evidence toward a Theory of Suggestion," *American Journal of Sociology* (1979), vol. 84, no. 5, pp. 1150–1174.

Page 224.
V. R. Ashton and S. Donnan, "Suicide by burning as an epidemic phenomenon: An analysis of 82 deaths and inquests in England and Wales in 1978–79, *Psychological Medicine* (1981), vol. 11, pp. 735–739.

Page 225.
Norman Kreitman, Peter Smith, and Eng-Seong Tan, "Attempted Suicide as Language: An Empirical Study," *British Journal of Psychiatry* (1970), vol. 116, pp. 465–473.

Page 230.
H. J. Eysenck. *Smoking, Health and Personality* (New York: Basic Books, 1965), p. 80. This reference is found in David Krogh's *Smoking: The Artificial Passion*, p. 107.

The statistics on smoking and sexual behavior come from: H. J. Eysenck, *Smoking, Personality and Stress* (New York: Springer-Verlag, 1991), p. 27.

Page 231.
David Krogh, *Smoking: The Artificial Passion*. (New York: W. H. Freeman, 1991).

Page 234.
Ovide Pomerleau, Cynthia Pomerleau, Rebecca Namenek, "Early Experiences with Tobacco among Women Smokers, Ex-smokers, and Never-smokers," *Addiction* (1998), vol. 93, no. 4, pp. 595–601.

Page 235.
Saul Shiffman, Jean A. Paty, Jon D. Kassel, Mary ann Gnys, and Monica Zettler-Segal, "Smoking Behavior and Smoking History of Tobacco Chippers," *Experimental and Clinical Psychopharmacology* (1994), vol. 2, no. 2, p. 139.

Page 239.
Judith Rich Harris, *The Nurture Assumption*.

Page 242.
David C. Rowe, *The Limits of Family Influence* (New York: Guilford Press, 1994). Rowe has a very good summary of the twins and adoption work.

Page 244.
Alexander H. Glassman, F. Stetner, B. T. Walsh et al., "Heavy smokers, smoking cessation, and clonidine: results of a double-blind, randomized trial," *Journal of the American Medical Association* (1988), vol. 259, pp. 2863–2866.

Page 246.
Alexander H. Glassman, John E. Helzer, Lirio Covey et al., "Smoking, Smoking Cessation, and Major Depression," *Journal of the American Medical Association* (1990), vol. 264, pp. 1546–1549.

Page 247.
Wendy Fidler, Lynn Michell, Gillian Raab, Anne Charlton, "Smoking: A Special Need?" *British Journal of Addiction* (1992), vol. 87, pp. 1583–1591.

Page 249.
The Neal Benowitz/Jack Henningfield strategy has been described in two places. Neal L. Benowitz and Jack Henningfield, "Establishing a nicotine threshold for addiction," *New England Journal of Medicine* (1994), vol. 331, pp. 123–125. Also: Jack Henningfield, Neal Benowitz, and John Slade, "Report to the American Medical Association: Reducing Illness and Death Caused by Cigarettes by Reducing Their Nicotine Content" (1997).

Page 251.
There is a good summary of the available statistics on drug use and addiction in: Dirk Chase Eldredge, *Ending the War on Drugs* (Bridgehampton, New York: Bridge Works Publishing, 1998), pp. 1–17.

Rubinstein, "Epidemic Suicide Among Micronesian Adolescents," p. 664.

Acknowledgments

The Tipping Point grew out of an article I wrote as a free-lancer for Tina Brown at the *New Yorker,* who ran the piece and then — to my surprise and delight — hired me. Thank you, Tina. She and her successor, David Remnick, graciously allowed me to spend many months away from the magazine to work on this book. The earliest draft of my manuscript was brilliantly critiqued by Terry Martin, now of Harvard University and formerly of our hometown of Elmira, who has been a source of intellectual inspiration to me since tenth-grade biology. I also owe special thanks to the extraordinary contributions of Judith Rich Harris, author of *The Nurture Assumption,* which changed the way I thought about the world, and my mother, Joyce Gladwell, who is and always will be my favorite writer. Judith Shulevitz, Robert McCrum, Zoe Rosenfeld, Jacob Weisberg, and Deborah Needleman took the time to read my manuscript and share their thoughts. DeeDee Gordon (and Sage) and Sally Horchow graciously lent me their homes for the long weeks of writing. I hope someday to return the favor. At Little, Brown, I had the pleasure of working with a team of talented and dedicated and wonderful professionals: Katie Long, Betty Power, Ryan Harbage, Sarah Crichton, and, most of all, my editor, Bill Phillips. Bill read this book so many times he can probably recite it by memory, and every time he read it his insight and intelligence made it a better book. Thank you. Two people, finally, have my deepest gratitude. First my agent and friend Tina Bennett, who conceived of this project and saw it through — protecting, guiding, helping, and inspiring me every step of the way. And second, my editor at the *New Yorker,* the incomparable Henry Finder, to whom I owe more than I can say. Thank you all.

Index